Immigrant Manifesto - Mindset of the Corporate Migrant

Obi Odenigbo

ISBN: 978-1-7331176-0-9

Book Designed by Acepub

Acknowledgements

I would like to thank two special ladies—Hiba and Gold. This book could not have been completed without their brilliant critiques and inspiration.

I would also like to acknowledge all hard-working migrants, who left their homes, and braced the adventure of actualizing their God-given dreams.

Above all, I would love to acknowledge the source and author of all knowledge, inspiration and wisdom.

Introduction

"I cannot teach anybody anything. I can only make them think."

- Socrates

The electronic copy of this book is listed for under a dollar, in order to make it more accessible to the intended audience. It is also intentionally limited to seven short chapters for two reasons. First, I wish to eliminate the excuse of not having enough time to get through it. Secondly, you might want to refer to it now and again—in order to imbibe the principles enshrined therein.

This book does not claim any literary excellence or genius. It is a simple guide that got me from making about ten dollars an hour to a six figure income in just five years. It also transformed me from a clueless and insecure immigrant to chapter president of the International Council of Systems Engineers. It's one thing to make money in a foreign country, it's another to gain personal fulfillment and professional growth *while* making money. The principles in this book will help you achieve both, by presenting logical strategies that will make you a success. It is often said that the opposite of success is failure. I disagree. The true opposite of success is going with the flow—or what you call, conformity. You do things because your friends and coworkers are doing it—not because you know why or believe in it. In order to be truly successful, you must develop a winning mindset along with a well thought out plan of attack. This book proposes steps you can take to achieve these.

Each of the seven chapters of this book contains true stories (sometimes with altered names to protect the identity of those involved) that demonstrate core principles. In turn, each principle is broken down into very simple yet practical steps (or disciplines) that worked for me multiple times with different companies. They did not only work for me, but for friends I shared them with. It is therefore my conviction that anyone can follow these tried and tested principles and—just like science—achieve similar outcomes within the same timeframe. It is not my intention to restrict the pathway to corporate success to the principles provided in this book. Instead, the intent is to offer an intellectual framework that worked for me, so as to assist you with the exercise of sound judgment in attaining your success.

While the primary audience of this book is the African migrant, this book will prove super useful to anyone looking to succeed in corporate America or in any workforce in the 'developed world'. It would also come handy to employers seeking to understand the mindset of African immigrants and how best to leverage our unique perspectives and behavioral norms. More importantly, it is my little way of sowing seeds of excellence and sound judgment into the future leaders of our society.

Prologue

"Diversity is being invited to the party. Inclusion is being asked to dance."

- Verna Myers

There is little question that one of the most divisive themes in the developed world today is immigration. Scroll down on your social media feed, turn on your TV or radio or just talk to others.

Questions about color and migration permeate the very fabric of our consciousness.

The economic condition back home, in sub-Saharan Africa, feeds this narrative. Every year, our colleges churn out tens of thousands of graduates who compete for quickly exhausting opportunities. This has led to a spike in crime rates, suicide, corruption, slavery and the brain drain to the West (Europe, Asia, Australia and North America).

Here, in the West, the debate on how immigrants add value to the workforce is a common one. Several commentaries on diversity and inclusion have been penned. Pretending that there are no differences between immigrants and natives only fuels this debate. The real question for corporations—and society—is how to leverage diversity and create an inclusive workforce. When this question is ignored, 'excluded' groups usually react in three ways: Get By, Get Out or Get Even.

These reactions cost corporations tens of millions of dollars in reputation damage, litigation, and a demotivated workforce. The list goes on and on. It is therefore understandable why smart corporations have started investing heavily in inclusion. However, in spite of these investments, African migrants still face significant hurdles in acclimatizing. I know this firsthand. And my experiences birthed this book.

Most literature on diversity and inclusion focuses on what employers can do to create a welcoming and inclusive atmosphere. And it feels like the onus of inclusion is exclusively on the employer or management. This philosophy is inherently flawed.

In this book, I focus on the mindset the immigrant needs to have—or avoid—in order to be successful. For instance, integrity is everything, even in small things—*especially* in small things. An employee who shows up habitually late may have plausible reasons for this (such as lack of adequate childcare or reliable transportation). But they unwittingly send the message: "I cannot be relied upon," "You cannot trust me."

I hope that by sharing the lessons I have learned, you will see more clearly the role of having the right mindset in revolutionizing the fate of your career. And, hopefully, you are motivated to form a systematic plan of action to navigate the waters of corporate America.

Contents

CHAPTER 1

Dispelling the African Time Syndrome

"What a damned Epicurean rascal is this! My heart is ready to crack with impatience... better three hours too soon than a minute too late. Fie, fie, fie!"

- William Shakespeare in the play, Merry Wives of Windsor

Imagine you were given $86,400 every morning and you were free to spend it as you chose. The only caveat is that at the end of the day, you would have to give up whatever is left of that money. How would you spend it? Would you waste it or be deliberate with your purchases? Would you rest easy knowing you made the best investments?

Well, that is pretty much what we are given every day. Except that, in our case, it's time, not Dollars.

And time is infinitely more valuable than any currency.

In the grand scheme of things, money isn't even second on the list. Time, Health—mental and physical—and Power all rank ahead of money. It is therefore much more costly to waste time than it is to waste money.

The black man has, over time, been perceived to be a sworn enemy of time. This perception is usually termed "black people time" or "African time". Back home in Nigeria, it isn't uncommon for people to show up two hours late for an event. As a matter of fact, it is almost socially acceptable to do so. Both the BBC and the International Journal of Cross-Cultural Management have published exposés on the African time problem. Unfortunately, this perception of lateness does not end in social settings, but follows through to the corporate world.

I was warned about this perception by my first roommate, Ike, who was also Nigerian. He laughed when I told him I would never be late to work.

"Bros, I dey tell you, e dey our blood," he said sarcastically. "We don even infect Oyinbo so tey dem don dey late pass us."

In other words:

"Our lateness, as a people, runs deep like blood in our veins. So much so that we infect even the white people we come in contact with, with this lateness."

I made a resolution to be the African who was never late.

At the time, I had just accepted a job offer and would be starting the following week. I did not have a car and lived about sixty miles away from my workplace. In order to actualize this resolution, I would have to ride two buses and a train and make it in before the 8 a.m. training. I also lived on Ike's couch. He was single, like me, and sometimes would have friends stay late into the wee hours of the morning, disrupting my sleep.

Many young people venturing into corporate America share a similar reality. Near impossible commutes, too many distractions from internal and external sources. And, like me, they may be surrounded by people whose lifestyles and habits pose some difficulty to their success. And if they are assertive enough to confront them, their relationships could suffer.

These are obstacles that you have to overcome.

Over time, I have learned to confront my problems square on. I find that a great place to start in this problem confrontation process is the articulation of the problem. Writing it down helps. Lateness. Indiscipline. Lack of courage. Whatever it is, write down the problem. Yes, on paper. When I share this, some of my friends give me the *is-something-wrong-with-this-guy* look. But I have seen the immense power of this simple "trick".

On a rare quiet evening, while seated in the living room of Ike's Brooklyn Park apartment, I decided to write down some plans I had been ruminating on. I got a sheet of paper and drew a line in the middle. On the left side, I wrote down my problems:

Getting to work in Eagan from Brooklyn Park before 8 AM.

Late visitors

No car

On the right side of the paper, I started to scribble down what felt like common sense solutions:

Set phone alarm for ~~4:00 AM~~ 4:15 AM

Talk to Ike about Irene and other visitors

Google Maps

Then onto the brainstorming, modification and execution of the plan. I picked up my phone and Googled the distance to Eagan. Google spat out the duration by driving, public commute, riding on a bicycle and even walking. I clicked on the public commute icon and it showed that it would take two hours and twenty minutes to get to Eagan! While I was not surprised, it dampened my spirit. But this also meant I could sleep for another fifteen minutes and still make the bus. So, I tweaked my solutions:

Set phone alarm for ~~4:00 AM 4:15 AM~~ 4:30 AM

Talk to Ike about Irene and other visitors

Google Maps

Waking up early was no fun, but my body quickly got used to it.

Proving that I was not subject to African time was only one motivation—I also needed the livelihood my work provided. My sister and mother had paid for my plane ticket to America and had given me a quickly exhausting sum. And there was a machismo part of me that wanted to pay them back sooner than later.

The buses in the Twin Cities ran like clockwork and one could easily see the bus schedules on the MetroTransit site. It all felt so magically organized to me. My whole life, I had only known speeding buses conducted by yelling young men hanging dangerously from open doors and announcing bus routes. Each bus route and fare dependent on the day's demand.

Here, it was easier to plan and I was never late for training. Even on those mornings when the Minneapolis snow storms caused me to want to stay in bed, or even disrupted the usual bus schedules.

The security guards at the front desk knew me as the first person to show up at work.

"Damn it, man! Do you ever sleep?!" they would ask playfully as I swiped my badge and walked into the building.

"Never!" I would chuckle. "Good Morning."

They were friendly, but nosy. I was surprised by how often they tried to steer our little morning chit chats into personal conversations. I guess it is part of their job to report suspicious behaviors and their other observations. And maybe they played a part in my being known as the African guy who was always on time.

My regard for time laid the foundation for some of the successes I enjoyed with the company. I was perceived as dependable and I knew it. I knew it from being progressively given more responsibilities. And within three years, I tripled my income within the same company! I could then afford an apartment by myself and I got one only five minutes away from work.

I would like to say I planned all this from the get-go, but I did not. It was not sheer luck either. It started with writing down my problems and pushing myself to solve them.

Of course, I needed the money and to prove myself in my new environment. However, in the process, I discovered the immense value of timeliness. Timeliness confers the perception of dependability. It opens doors that wits cannot. It destroys century-old prejudices that words alone cannot erase. It is the baptism of legitimate success.

The successes that followed have convinced me that this principle of valuing your time—and other people's time—is the foundation for success in corporate America. This is also true of all relationships—personal or professional. It doesn't matter if you are the smartest, the most gifted or the hardest worker. Without practicing the simple principle of managing your time wisely, you cannot reach your full potential. This has been the bane of so many hard-working talents whom I have worked with.

Think of it this way—would you entrust your money to the care of a bank that you know would waste it? How then can you confer respect and moral authority upon yourself if you do not value the most important resource of those you interact with? People who are not punctual are stereotyped as incapable of keeping commitments. Very few corporations will entrust extra responsibilities—or promotions—to anyone they cannot rely upon to keep time commitments.

I had a colleague named Phil—an exceptionally smart African American who started with the company a couple of months before I did. It was a call center and he did so well in such a short time that he was selected to mentor me. To be a mentor so early in his time with the company spoke volumes of his work ethic. I respected him and he reminded me several times to stop calling him *sir*. It was a hard thing to stop. Growing up in Nigeria, we were taught never to call older people or people in authority by their first names. We used "sir" or "ma" or sometimes even prefixed their names with "uncle" and "aunty", even if they were not related to us.

I shadowed Phil to learn and would sit and listen to him talk to customers on the phone. He handled their concerns expertly and easily navigated the multiple applications on his computer. He would never raise his voice at angry customers, even when they yelled and cursed at him. Most times, he would get them singing his praises by the end of the call. Phil was a customer service genius, a computer wizard, an enchanting sweet-talker and the best multi-tasker I had ever seen. He was evidently talented. However, Phil was typically five to ten minutes late.

He had a daughter whom he dropped off at school before coming to work. Sometimes, he got held up in traffic or forgot his badge at home and would need to drive back to go get it.

"It's my daughter's school again," he would say. "And I forgot my badge. Had to drive back in that traffic."

"It's okay. Hope you're not going to get into trouble," I would respond. "You can tell the manager that you were delayed at your daughter's school and had to go back."

"Nah. You're good if you punch in within ten minutes of your shift," he would say. "It's when you're an hour late or don't show up at all that you're in trouble".

Phil's lateness continued to worsen.

While he always had compelling reasons to be late, he—and so many others—became known for their lateness.

Six or seven months after I started with the company, I became Phil's manager. He was graceful enough to congratulate and work with me. But he couldn't hide his bitterness, sometimes even calling me out in front of others. In fairness, he knew the job—the product, processes and the technology—better than I did. He often murmured about how much smarter he was and that was probably true too. Some agents on my team complained to me about how much he was undermining my authority and advised that I should do something. But I let him enjoy the small, momentary victories.

"What does a brother need to do to get ahead here?" he eventually asked me one day when we were both having lunch in the cafeteria. "Obi, I've worked hard. I've put in work, bro. You know this, man. I've put in blood, sweat and tears. You know, Obi!"

"I know, Phil."

"So tell me what I gotta do, bro. I come in on the weekends, I do OT. I have trained many people here. Hell, I trained you!"

"I know, Phil," I muttered again.

"Like what do I gotta do, Obi? It's just frustrating. They promoted Lindsey last week. *Lindsey* who I trained and even took supervisor calls for. She knows nothing! I don't mean to sound like a hater, but she's dumb. Very dumb, bro, and you know this. They just keep promoting their people."

I looked at him and my eyes asked if I was also one of "their people". However, he clarified:

"No offense, bro, but they look at people from the Motherland differently. They like you more than they like us. They don't look at Africans the way they look at us. That's why you're the only one in leadership. They hate us, bro. But they hate us more than they hate you."

This was the first time I gave real thought to the distinctions within the black race in America. His characterization concerned me, but not as much as figuring out how something as seemingly trivial as lateness could explain such talent not being promoted. He had given so much to the company and really needed the raise.

After our lunch, I scheduled a meeting with a fellow manager, Kristal. We had become close; she was my mentor in my new role. I also trusted her enough to share my concerns about Phil's stagnancy. She agreed to meet at the local Denny's the same evening.

Kristal explained certain truths in a way only Kristal could. Her experience and honesty opened my eyes.

In a nutshell, being late sends a series of messages—not subtle, but *loud* messages.

"I am more important than your schedule."

"I cannot honor my commitments."

"I do not care about your time."

"I cannot be relied upon."

"I am that 'black people' stereotype you heard about."

She did not use the exact words in the last sentence, but I got the gist. I made sure to communicate to Phil what I got from that conversation.

Now that we have settled the significance of valuing time, it is important to spend the last part of this chapter helping you understand how to apply this principle. While consistently being late is rude, consistent punctuality shows tremendous respect for people's most valuable resource—their time. And to be consistently punctual requires personal discipline (such as setting an alarm clock on your phone) and proper planning (such as scribbling notes and using Google Maps).

There is abundant research on the power of visualization. In a neuroscience article by Mark Murphy titled "Neuroscience Explains Why You Need To Write Down Your Goals If You Actually Want To Achieve Them", he argues that writing down your goals is strongly associated with goal success.

In a study titled "What They Don't Teach You in the Harvard Business School" conducted on Harvard MBAs in 1979, a simple question was posed:

"Have you set clear, written goals for your future and made plans to accomplish them?"

The response from the survey showed that:

- Eighty-four percent of the MBA students didn't have specific goals
- Thirteen percent of them had goals but no formal method of committing to them
- Three percent had clearly written goals.

Ten years later, in 1989, the same group of graduates were interviewed by the same researchers. The three percent with clearly written goals were making ten times more money than the other ninety-seven percent of their classmates combined!

This is no accident. Planning is crucial to success. Research after research has shown that you are twenty to forty percent more likely to achieve your goals when they are written down, than when not.

It all comes down to three simple disciplines:

1. Plan in a realistic way. Do not underestimate the time you spend in your morning routine. Know how long it takes you to get out of bed and ready for work. Then have a good idea of your commute time. Google Maps is a handy, excellent tool. You also have to understand yourself and how you function. You need to know how much sleep you need to prepare you for the next day—or just how much coffee you need to function.
2. Be okay with buffer-time. It's always better to come too early than to risk being late. In my early days, I sometimes arrived up to an hour before work started. And while I was not getting paid for that hour, I made peace with it. I saw it as an investment in my professional growth. If you wish to succeed in corporate America, you should be comfortable with such buffer-time. Besides being a professional investment, having some "me time" is beneficial. With it, you can afford to review the events and lessons from the previous day and plan your day before others get in.
3. If it is not written down, it will not be solved. As mentioned earlier, there is a lot of research that validates the power of visualization. Put it in writing or on your virtual calendar. Otherwise, you risk being a poor steward of your time and that of others.

Making punctuality a habit translates to:

"I can honor my commitments."

"I am very reliable."

"I am trustworthy."

"I am prepared for the unexpected."

"I value this job."

"I can be trusted and entrusted with more responsibilities."

Philip Stanhope, the fourth Earl of Chesterfield, couldn't have put this any better when he said:

"Know the true value of time; snatch, seize, and enjoy every moment of it. No idleness, no laziness, and no procrastination. Never put off till tomorrow what you can do today."

Transgression of this principle:

In October of 2003, international journalists in the United Kingdom were kept waiting by the king of Ghana's largest ethnic group who was visiting Alexandra Palace in North London. It was the climax of a Ghanaian trade exhibition titled "Ghana Expo 2003". The journalists had been informed that Otumfuo Osei Tutu II from the Ashanti people would arrive at the exhibition at eleven a.m. The time was later changed to 2 p.m., but the king did not show up until two hours later when the journalists had already left after waiting for so long. The incident limited the exposure the exhibition could have had and further reinforced the unfortunate narrative that Africans are terrible time-keepers.

Brazilian soccer star Adriano Leite Ribiero was tipped to be the next 'Ronaldo' in football. His talent, skill and goal scoring abilities were so incredible that in the early 2000s, he averaged a goal every other game. Every soccer enthusiast understands how incredible this feat is. However, in the prime of his career, at only twenty-seven, Adriano started showing up late for training and partying a lot. He developed a reputation for being unreliable and got traded from club to club. Despite his indisputable talent, no club in Europe wanted to sign him. So he returned to Brazil, his home country. There he joined Corinthians football club where he was famously fined ten percent of his salary for being repeatedly late. In 2012, he joined Flamengo, another football club in Brazil, but made no appearances for them. Adriano is a classic example of an amazing talent who was doomed by a lack of discipline, a reputation for unreliability and overall abysmal time management.

Observance of this principle:

Charles Dickens, the greatest writer of the Victorian era and author of books such as "Oliver Twist" and "Great Expectations" was notoriously meticulous about time and planning. He kept to a military-strict schedule; always writing in his study between 9 a.m. and 2 p.m. before taking three-hour walks. He demanded complete silence in his house during his work hours, and required that his pens, ink and a small collection of statuettes be specially arranged on his desk to help him think. Dickens' bizarre habits are said to have extended to his bedroom as he only slept facing north, believing that it better aligned him to the electrical currents of the earth. It is widely believed that this attention to schedule and time helped him churn out the fifteen great novels that made him the legend he was, while maintaining his commitments as a journalist, editor, illustrator and anti-slavery activist.

CHAPTER 2

Servant Leadership

"Everybody can be great ... because anybody can serve. You don't have to have a college degree to serve. You don't have to make your subject and verb agree to serve. You only need a heart full of grace. A soul generated by love."

- Martin Luther King Jr.

Kristal's team had the best Average Handle Time—or AHT—in the company. They had the best sales numbers and checked all the boxes in other productivity metrics in our call center, Trinitas. The "Manager of the Month" plaque sat on her desk for three months in a row. And her team members were regular winners of the "Employee of the Month" award. Kristal had a knack for taking the newbies placed on her team from edgy to bona fide sales agents in little time. She was a superstar!

Her success bred jealousy among the other managers. I even overheard some of them talk about how her performance would suffer if her team were shuffled because—according to them—"she was only lucky to have smart agents". But it wasn't luck—there was a je ne sais quoi about Kristal that I was determined to find out and learn.

Becoming a team manager—and a success-thirsty one—forced me to realize and confront a bias I didn't even know I held. Growing up in Nigeria, I was used to seeing men in leadership roles—the politicians, the professors, the priests and other authority figures were mostly men. So, automatically, I found Kristal's excellence a bit jarring. However, with this bias, I was almost certain I could best her if I tried. So I chose Kristal as my mentor—shadowing and studying her.

The first thing that stared me in the face was how highly engaged her team was. Working, for them, was fun. Somehow, Kristal incorporated her own ingenious versions of Monopoly and Word Kraft into the achievement of set targets. And she showed her agents how valuable they were by being, literally, at their beck and call. She answered a million questions, jumped on complaint calls immediately and rarely missed her weekly one-on-one meetings with each agent. She also planned extensively and had her daily goals pinned to her desk. And she took responsibility, never pointing an accusatory finger at her agents.

"Sometimes—and not all the time, guys—but sometimes, agents' mistakes are as a result of training or managerial defects, and not the agent's doing ..." I heard her quip in more than one staff meeting.

I remember her jumping on a call where the agent was in tears and defending the agent:

"Chloe was just trying to protect your account information, ma'am," she explained to the customer. "She is restricted by GDPR laws on what information she can proactively provide and that's why she could not give you the address listed on your account ... Have you lived in any other place besides the Manhattan address you gave her?"

Once I was given a team; I tried to emulate Kristal's leadership style, but it was harder than I thought. I started by trying to learn Monopoly and other popular American board games, so as to link goals to games like Kristal did.

It was useless.

They were not the WHOT and Ludo of my Nigerian childhood. And even though I learnt them, I could not communicate as well with them as Kristal could.

Then, one morning on the elevator, we bumped into each other and engaged in small talk. She ended the conversation in typical fashion: asking if I needed her help with anything.

This time, I took her up on the offer—and asked what her secret was.

"What's your secret, Kristal? It can't just be the games. How do you make them hit such numbers? What's the secret?"

She smiled into my eyes. "There is no secret, Obi. You just need to be a servant."

"A servant?" I asked. "What do you mean, servant? I'm their manager. I have to lead and motivate them to perform like I did when I was an agent."

"Yes. But their performance depends on how you do it. You should serve to lead ..."

Having the words "serve" and "lead" in the same sentence sounded contradictory. In my experience, leaders in different spheres of life—parents, teachers, professors, pastors, elders, managers, politicians—were bosses, not servants. They were revered, nay feared, and listened to. Not the other way around.

Kristal made me realize that I didn't need to copy her games or schedule adherence techniques. It was all about the mindset—and I needed to change mine to one of service.

"You have to look at yourself and your title differently. Our people are our greatest assets. And we have to make them feel that way. You have to make them feel that way." She reiterated.

The concept of servant leadership stems from Jesus of Nazareth's model of leadership and there is a fascinating story of how he spells it out. Two of Jesus' disciples, James and John, who were brothers, approached him about being made his right-hand men when he attained kingship. They wanted power and honor. Quite naturally, learning about this request sparked outrage among the other members of Jesus' close circle. Notice that this fight was not about money, but about power and authority.

Jesus calmed the waters by saying:

"The rulers of the world have great power. Their important officials give many orders to people. You must not behave like that. Whoever wants to become great among you must be your servant. Whoever wants to be important must be a slave of all."

This proposes that service of those under and around you is crucial to your greatness. This is the guiding principle behind great people like Nelson Mandela, Martin Luther King, Bill Gates and even Ronald Reagan. There is unanimity among the business elite that this philosophy brings out the best in others and many a research has shown this to be true. The mindset also has to match the attitude. For example: if I take over a problematic call from an agent begrudgingly, I may resolve the immediate issue, but I am no servant leader—the begrudging attitude defeats the spirit of servant leadership.

You may wonder how servant leadership can apply to someone who is not in a leadership position. But there are little everyday opportunities for this in things like listening to and encouraging others, helping to clean up after a party or helping someone move. It really is a mindset of uplifting people that necessarily shows itself through actions.

Think about it this way—the biggest hurdle is convincing yourself mentally that your most important job, is serving others. Once you convince yourself of this, the outward manifestation of servant leadership becomes natural.

Two months after that eye-opening conversation with Kristal, I won the "Manager of the Month" award.

"You did it, Obi!" Kristal cheered when my name was called out.

"Go Obi!" The whole meeting joined in.

"Come on, Obi. Smile!" another manager echoed.

I complied, flashing a wide grin, as I posed with my certificate and plaque for a picture with the Site Director.

It meant the world.

I remember leaving the cafeteria where the award was presented and making my way to one of the many empty conference rooms down the hall. It was there that I celebrated with words of affirmation, laughter and multiple dabs, tucking my face into the crook of my right arm and flinging the other arm towards the ceiling.

I couldn't be more grateful to Kristal. She was a consummate planner and time manager and was generous enough to share so much of herself with me. And I learned, especially, that while I couldn't be as good as she was in board games or in delivering witty bits of motivation, I could plan and prioritize to make more time for my team. This is an important link—good time management aids effective servant leadership. Both principles have to go hand in hand. To truly serve others, you have to value their most important resource—time.

This is why it is necessary that we dealt with the importance of time management in the first chapter.

At work, I spent my first fifteen minutes doing desk rounds—asking agents little things, like how their nights went or about their morning commutes. I would also ask if they needed anything and write down their feedback. I could tell that they appreciated the interest I showed in their wellbeing. After that, I would go to my desk and pull up my calendar to see what meetings were planned for the day. This helped me sequence my work for the day. At the end of the day, I would reacquaint myself with my team, especially those with whom I'd had no special interaction with during the day. This was crucial to surviving the chaos of the call center.

It all comes down to the following disciplines:

1. Practice time management (see Chapter One).
2. Convince yourself that the most important part of your job is service to your coworkers.
3. Actively listen to your peers and seek new ways to serve.

In conclusion, it is important to point out that servant leadership can sometimes be thankless. People will think you are foolish and try to either take advantage of you or talk you into their "wisdom". Ignore any such contrary opinion and persevere in service of those around you. That being said, it is important that you find a balance as you still have a job to do. Servant leaders are not doormats and should therefore look after themselves.

This subtlety is addressed in the next chapter.

Transgression of this principle:

The latter part of the fifteenth century witnessed the reign of Pope Alexander VI, who is regarded by many as one of the most evil popes of all time. Instead of advancing the servant leadership principles advocated by Jesus Christ, whose seat he figuratively occupied, Alexander advanced his greed and personal gratification. He infamously married off his beautiful daughter, Lucrezia, to Giovanni Sforza for a large dowry. However, he eventually annulled the marriage because, as Pope, he wielded such authority. He then married her off to Duke Alfonso of Aragon in order to exploit a favorable political opportunity. And when he realized that the marriage had lost its political advantage, he conspired to have the poor duke killed in August of 1500. Pope Alexander then married her off, for the third time, to the duke of Ferrara to consolidate his political gains. He cared very little for the Church or for Rome, threw tons of extravagant parties, confiscated money from the wealthy and was anything but a servant leader. Many historians believe he was poisoned by his son, Cesare, although other historians debate his exact cause of death. Either way, Pope Alexander VI is the anti-thesis of servant leadership and will go down in history as one of the worst men to occupy the seat of St. Peter.

Lance Armstrong attained legendary status for winning the Tour de France seven consecutive times from 1999 to 2005. Given how difficult it is to compete in this event, Lance soon became a legend. However, all his wins were voided in 2012 when an investigation proved that he had used performance-enhancing drugs. His self-serving hypocrisy led him to crave victory at the expense of his peers who put in their blood, sweat and tears into those difficult races. He eventually received a lifetime ban from all sports that use the World Anti-Doping Code, which effectively ended his career.

President Nixon is an ironic example of the importance of the principle of Servant Leadership. After a long career of service, which included serving in the House of Representatives, the Senate, and as Vice President, Nixon was elected president in 1968. His reputation and career of 'service' to the American people, appeared solid and impeccable. However, during his reelection campaign in 1972, Nixon's administration bugged the offices of his political opponents to sabotage them and gain an unfair advantage. When the Watergate scandal came to light, President Nixon was disgraced out of office.

Observance of this principle:

Martin Luther King Jr thoroughly embodies the principle of servant leadership. His ability to listen, empathize and persuade people to buy into his vision of equality, was second to none. He was able to dialogue with his enemies and successfully converted many of those who disagreed with him with his sound logic, soul-searching criticisms and empathetic demeanor. He famously taught that everyone had the potential for greatness, because greatness is determined by service, and anyone could serve. Such words were accompanied by concrete actions such as non-violent protests as well as heart-rending speeches. His legendary status as servant leader was solidified as he ultimately gave his life in service of humanity on April 4, 1968 at the hands of an assassin. Before his tragic death, he insisted, that at his funeral, there should be no mention of his awards (including his PhD and Nobel Peace Prize) or any other honors he received during his life. His exact words in reference to his funeral, capture the essence of his servant leadership disposition:

"Tell them not to mention that I have a Nobel Peace Prize – that isn't important. Tell them not to mention that I have three or four hundred other awards – that's not important. Tell them not to mention where I went to school... I'd like somebody to mention that

day that Martin Luther King, Jr., tried to give his life serving others. I'd like for somebody to say that day that Martin Luther King, Jr., tried to love somebody. I want you to be able to say that day that I did try to feed the hungry. And I want you to be able to say that day that I did try in my life to clothe those who were naked. I want you to say on that day that I did try in my life to visit those who were in prison. I want you to say that I tried to love and serve humanity."

CHAPTER 3
Self-Confidence

"Never forget for an instant that this is a perfect world, and that you are a god among gods. You are as great as the greatest, but all are your equals."

- Wallace D Wattles

Now that you have dispelled the notion of African time through methodic planning and have started to become a servant leader, you must now believe in your limitless power! Servant leadership without self-confidence will push you to servility, making you a doormat to be trampled upon at will.

While servant leadership calls for humility, it does not advocate servility.

Humility is a mindset of moderation in which one does not consider themselves as superior to the next person. Servility, on the other hand, is a mindset of excessive willingness to please others. It goes well beyond moderation. Like Wattles said, you must hold a viewpoint of yourself as a god among other gods. No one is inferior *or* superior to you.

This balance is subtle but very important.

A feeling of inferiority is a dangerous impediment to your success in any corporation. It waters down your efforts in time management and with developing a true servant leadership attitude. It stifles the realization of your full potential. Think about it this way; if people do not believe in you, you could work around their doubts, prove them wrong and still succeed. But with little to no belief in yourself, you put yourself at a significant disadvantage.

There is an Igbo adage that goes:

"Agwo emeghi nke o ji buru agwo, umuaka achiri ya hie nku."

Which translates to:

"If a snake doesn't use its venom, little kids will use it as a rope in tying up firewood."

This proverb exemplifies how a lack of knowledge or confidence in your strengths can severely diminish your potential and turn you into the doormat alluded to earlier. Like the ignorant snake, you do yourself a huge disservice by not fighting this feeling of inadequacy! This takes time and constant practice.

Starting out in America, my self-confidence was low. This is something I know that many other immigrants also contend with. How can we not? We are suddenly out of our place of comfort, and thrust into this fabled place with intimidating buildings, frigid weather and confusing social protocols. The accent is different, and communication can be daunting. Even though your first language is English and you speak and write it expertly. This language insecurity can accentuate your otherness and deflate self-confidence built over a lifetime.

For instance, on one of my early days in America, I walked into a small shop in South Minneapolis and did not find what I was looking to buy. Coming from a communal society, we are wired to make sure that we are seen as conforming to societal norms. I remember thinking it was rude to leave the store without buying or at least, offering an explanation to the salesperson on the counter. After about thirty minutes of mulling over what the right social protocol was, I bought an item that I had no need for.

Back at work, I could tell that my manager was growing tired of asking me to stop referring to him as "sir".

"Just call me Jeff," he would say.

It was hard for me to address him by his first name; as it seemed incredibly rude. However, the unlearning process of learning to refer to Jeff by his first name forced me to slowly evolve my thought patterns. I gradually came to terms with the fact that he was a person just like me. A god just like myself! I learned it was possible to show respect while viewing myself as equal to the recipient of this respect. This mental change was crucial to building my self-confidence and demystifying those in authority.

Once you start seeing those you aspire to become as equal to you, it breaks down pre-existing mental barriers, thus making attaining their positions of influence more realistic. Otherwise, your subconscious will keep whispering to you that your goals are unrealistic.

Something as trivial as calling Jeff by his first name was a breakthrough moment for me. The African culture places incredible value on reverence—especially for elders and people in authority. This sort of reverence borders on fear and an aversion for questioning authority. The great Nelson Mandela described this reverence in his autobiography—'Long Walk To Freedom'—when he wrote:

"Like all Xhosa children, I acquired knowledge mainly through observation. We were meant to learn through imitation and emulation, not through questions. When I first visited the homes of whites, I was often dumbfounded by the number and nature of questions that children

asked of their parents – and their parents' unfailing willingness to answer them. In my household, questions were considered a nuisance; adults imparted information as they considered necessary"

Mandela's observation resonates through most African societies. In addition, we were taught to offer up our seats if elders needed them. We were not to talk to them with pocketed hands or hands akimbo. And we were never to give them things with our left hands.

While arguably valuable, if left unchecked, these cultural norms could lead to inferiority complex and its attendant negative barriers.

At the other end of the confidence spectrum is the dysfunctional extreme of over-confidence – which borders on delusions of grandeur. I have worked with people who almost routinely belittle others because of their excessive confidence in their own abilities. This is not the sort of confidence I propose – and it can be just as damaging as the opposite extreme of servility. Applying moderation and balance will preserve you from both dysfunctional extremes.

When a managerial position opened up at work in 2013, I did not apply. I did not think I was good enough for the position. I remember the recruiter, Tyler, asking me if I had applied.

In response, I asked if he thought I could do it.

"Of course," he said

I did not believe him. He was a recruiter after all, so how could he know how I executed my functions? I was sure that he was only making conversation and being nice. And truly, it was nice to hear the validation in his voice, even if it wasn't sincere.

Kristal, my friend and mentor, also asked if I applied to

this same position at a different time. I was sure it was only flattery. And I wondered aloud if I was good enough to be a manager, with only a few months under my belt. Her yes was unequivocal. She even persuaded me to fill the application right away and helped me through the process.

"You have what it takes. They respect you here, Obi. We all do. You are professional, never late to work and always willing to assist everybody ..."

I tell this story to show how crippling a lack of confidence in one's self can be. It took the confidence of both Tyler and Kristal to convince myself that I was good enough to apply for the position. My practice of time management and servant leadership won me the faith of these two. And their faith in my abilities boosted my self-confidence. This is why I talk about self-confidence in the third chapter after time management and servant leadership have been discussed. The results from the practice of these two principles shows you and those around you—some of your potential, and in the process, adds blocks to your structure of self-confidence.

The first couple of weeks I had at my first job in the US were spent in training. And while I was thrilled at getting paid for just sitting in class, I became terrified when we started listening to the recordings of customer calls played in class. My perception about the civility of the civilized world was shattered. Here I was, listening to customers curse and use all sorts of expletives at the agents, who responded with persevered cordial professionalism. And these were agents with American accents. I shuddered at the thought of how these clients would eviscerate me and my thick West African accent.

After listening to one of the more disturbing calls, I walked up to Sherryl, the trainer, and told her I would be quitting at the end of the week.

"What are you talking about, Obi?" she said. "Come with me."

She took me to an empty conference room, turned the lights on, and I could see worry scowled on her face. She put her pen in the middle of her notepad, folded it and tossed it on the large shiny conference table.

"What's going on, Obi? Talk to me!"

I opened up about my concerns with my accent. Americans seem to talk faster when angry. And I told her how I wasn't ready to deal with angry clients whom I would struggle to understand, and who would not be patient enough to hear me. I told her it was a marriage made in hell and I wasn't going to wait around to be incinerated.

"Obi, I swear I can hear you clearly," she rebuffed. "You have an accent, but we all do! The guys on the East Coast don't speak like us here in the Midwest. And all you need to do is listen to folks from the South—those guys have thicker accents than you do."

"I don't know."

"I'm telling you. Have you heard them?"

I wasn't buying her argument but her steady, blue-eyed gaze and the wrinkles forming on her forehead conveyed genuine concern.

"Give it one month, Obi. Just one month. And if you still feel this way, I promise not to talk you out of it. You're always here on time, you're always paying attention in class and you're never loud like some of the others. You'll make a great agent, I promise you. Trust me on this one."

This was the first time someone in authority had shown me

such concern. It was a refreshing culture shock, and it made me feel seen and respected. This gesture persuaded me more than anything she said. Our conversation ended with my resolve to stick it out for a month and then take it from there.

The reason I tell both stories is to demonstrate the fact that I would not have made significant progress—despite being punctual, reliable and a servant leader—if I allowed my feelings of inferiority to get the better of me. Inferiority complex highlights compelling arguments in your head as to why you cannot succeed, while blurring weightier arguments as to why you can, if you try. This is what psychologists refer to as Cognitive Distortion. While not classified as a mental disorder, it is a mindset problem.

Cognitive Distortion can be so convincing and one-sided, that it is difficult for a person in this situation to recognize it as a mindset problem. And this is why counter arguments or validations from those around you are powerful. People around you can sometimes see the greatness that you don't see in yourself.

If someone made the proverbial snake aware of its power, chances are that it wouldn't let itself be reduced to a rope!

The ancient Romans understood this, as they used to say:

"Vox Populi, Vox Dei."

Which translates to:

"The voice of the people is the voice of God."

It highlights the importance of listening.

Another potent weapon against inferiority complex is faith. African migrants are generally religious and are largely Muslims and Christians.

Both religions are filled with scripture that calls for confidence and faith in one's source—i.e. God. Cognizance of both your source and your resource—i.e. abilities—can be a potent combination in boosting your self-worth. The importance of the knowledge of one's source is exemplified by individuals who go through pains, spending lots of time and money, in order to find their biological parents. Many of them feel incomplete or empty without this knowledge. That feeling of emptiness sometimes affects their confidence, self-worth and ability to forge meaningful relationships. On the other hand, if you have ever seen a real prince or princess walk into a room, you would agree that they barely need any introduction. The confidence and poise they exude is almost palpable. Something about the way they carry themselves radiates nobility, grace and captures the attention of their audience. I'm convinced that if you knew you were royal; that awareness would translate to your conduct, confidence and overall savoir faire. The internalization of your royalty status will instill an insane amount of confidence in you. The ability of royals—or confident people—to capture their audience has less to do with their wealth, as it has to do with the knowledge of who, and whose, they are. This knowledge of their roots and source is directly responsible for the confidence they emit. Religion or spirituality can have a similar effect with overcoming inferiority complex.

The Prophet Muhammed, peace be upon him, once said:

"The greatest jihad is to battle your own soul, to fight the evil within yourself."

In this context, the evil within us is inferiority complex. In life, as well as in the corporate world, this feeling of inferiority kills growth. And growth—spiritual growth, emotional growth, financial growth, intellectual growth—is arguably the primary reason for our existence.

A defeatist mindset also discourages openness. And without opening up, help cannot come in. I keep wondering what would have happened if I did not open up to Sherryl. This is the rationale behind exit interviews. Everyone is heard and helped. As a migrant in corporate America, it is important to always be honest about your concerns and thus give yourself the opportunity to win this battle of your own soul.

The Bible has this line from one of Israel's great kings, King David:

"The Lord is my light and my salvation. Whom shall I fear? The Lord is the stronghold of my life. Before whom shall I shrink?"

Such assertions of strength and courage can do wonders when truly internalized by the migrant worker. There is no one to shrink from or be afraid of. Not the prince, nor the white man, nor the pauper.

Whatever your religious persuasion, it helps to spend time reading books that enrich your self-worth and faith. Spiritual growth will usually accompany emotional growth and thus self-confidence. Write down passages from these books that remind you of your greatness and your innate abilities. These words are therapeutic. Tell yourself over and over again that God is with you. That he is guiding you and empowering you to do all things—and with time, you will find yourself getting rid of the inferior mindset.

And even if you have no religious inclinations, positive affirmations have been demonstrated by numerous research studies to be very effective. There is ample research—from James Vicary in the 1950's to the Yale Studies of the 2000's—that support the power of suggestive articulation and subliminal affirmations. However, they are outside the scope of this book. The power doesn't lie as much in the words as it does in your believing those words—and letting them permeate your subconscious. By repeating words that affirm your strength and success, you begin to subconsciously believe them.

Mohammed Ali understood the power of this concept, as he once said:

"I am the greatest! I said that even before I knew I was."

He privately affirmed his greatness and it took roots in his subconscious, before it manifested publicly in the different boxing arenas where his greatness was affirmed.

Finally, there is a case to be made for a correlation between self-confidence and physical fitness. Making time to stay healthy will boost your self-image and confidence. This is not to say that a lack of physical fitness should make you any less confident in who you are, however, keeping both mind and body healthy will do your confidence a world of good.

In summary, a lack of self-confidence is like running a marathon with a heavy bag on your back. You are unlikely to finish the marathon with your co-athletes running with no bags, let alone win the race. To compete favorably in the corporate marathon, you must let go of that baggage by adhering to the following principles and disciplines:

1. Methodic time management (See Chapter One)
2. Servant leadership (See Chapter Two)
3. Paying attention to external counter-arguments.
4. Faith
5. Physical fitness

Transgression of this principle:

The story of the great lawgiver, Moses, is central to Judaism,

Christianity, Islam and other Abrahamic religions. These religions record and observe the Ten Commandments given through him and hold Moses in great esteem. However, this great man had issues with his confidence and felt inadequate. This inadequacy is highlighted in his multiple excuses to God when urged to confront the Pharaoh and demand the liberation of the Jewish slaves. He highlighted his life-long issue with stuttering, according to this quote from the book of Exodus: 'Then Moses said to the LORD, "O my Lord, I am not eloquent, neither before nor since you have spoken to your servant; but I am slow of speech and slow of tongue."' He also brought up his insignificance in the face of such a mighty Egyptian King. He is quoted as saying, "Who am I that I should go to Pharaoh?" In other words, he did not think himself good enough to approach the Pharaoh. If Moses had not overcome this low self-esteem or lack of confidence, there is no question that his historical and theological significance would have been greatly diminished. He may not have become the great lawmaker we know him to be. The 'Mosaic' Laws and the famous Ten Commandments, which formed the bedrock for a lot of historical civilizations, may have come through a different man or woman. Thankfully, Moses overcame this impediment.

Observance of this principle:

King David contrasts with Moses when it comes to confidence and self-esteem. This confidence is highlighted in the famous Biblical and Islamic accounts of the young fearless shepherd boy, David (referred to as Daud in the Quran), who took on the six foot-nine warrior, Goliath (referred to as Jalut in the Quran). David had experience defending his cattle and herd from invading wild animals and poachers. However, what is more remarkable about the teenage boy was his confidence in his ability to transfer this 'stone-slinging' skill to defeating a seasoned combat warrior. His lack of war experience or physique did not dampen his conviction in his skill and the 'spirit' within him—i.e. his resource and his source. This courageous attitude was crucial to his many successes later in life. The famous battle ended with the defeat of the experienced giant and the cementing of David's legacy in the annals of history, mythology and theology.

CHAPTER 4

Know Yourself. Grow Yourself

"After climbing a great hill, one only finds that there are many more hills to climb. I have taken a moment here to rest, to steal a view of the glorious vista that surrounds me, to look back on the distance I have come. But I can only rest for a moment... and I dare not linger, for my walk is not ended."

- Nelson Mandela

My day was planned to a T in a chaotic call center environment. Until you work at one, it is tough to appreciate the enormity of this achievement. This time management mastery helped me become a better servant leader. I had time to meet with all my agents, conduct consistent one-on-one coaching and craft performance improvement plans. With each agent, I would play pre-recorded calls and they would tell me what they could have done better. Their self-scrutiny grew with each coaching session. In fact, they began to coach themselves and our meetings became mere formalities. They did ninety percent of the talking and analysis while I cheered them on like a fan.

In those sessions, we would decide what to work on the following week. Usually, we would come up with two goals for the following week. I learned that giving them more than two goals was unrealistic and overwhelming. So, I went with one goal for the agent and one for myself. These goals were also SMART, i.e. Specific, Measurable, Achievable, Result-focused and Time-bound. This helped keep us accountable and efficient with realizing our goals.

We started each coaching session by reviewing the status of the previous week's goals and concluded with phrases such as:

"Tell me what's in it for you if you ..."

"What would you gain by working on ...?"

You would be amazed at how many people improve from self-identifying rather than being told their flaws.

The SMART principle was not only applied to work goals, but to personal ones. I remember helping some of them apply to other positions, research ways to improve their credit scores and even review college applications and essays. They started seeing their jobs as having some meaning—they weren't just coming in for the money, they were making a difference in their lives and the lives of their customers.

It's extraordinary how this shift in mindset can unlock powers in these amazing people. I cannot tell you how many times I have seen low-performing agents become phenomenal professionals.

More agents were getting promoted from my team than from any other. The new IT personnel, John and Derek, the new trainer, Ali, and three other supervisors were all promoted from my team. I had won more "Manager of the Month" plaques than I knew what to do with and now commanded the respect and admiration of my colleagues.

However, in the midst of all this success, something was missing. I still felt inadequate. For some reason, I hadn't been able to shake off all the demons of inferiority that had followed me from Nigeria. And maybe they were not demons but that innate instinct in all of us to grow. The same impulse in caterpillars, plants, larva, kittens and babies.

Speaking of kittens and babies, isn't it curious that kittens do not grow into adult humans nor little babies into adult cats? Why is this so, even though a 2007 study by Pontius *et al.* of the Genome Research Lab shows a ninety percent similarity between the genes of domestic kittens and human babies?

I'll tell you why.

Our growth patterns are determined by information stored in our DNA. These tiny threads carry our genetic code. All of us develop and grow only by cracking this code. Otherwise, growth is not structured and becomes improbable.

Look at it this way: in order to grow naturally, our cells have learned to decode this God-written code. In the same way, in order to grow into successful people, we must learn to decode our God-given talents and inborn proclivities. It is therefore no surprise that the first discipline in the principle of structured growth is knowing yourself.

Our faiths are filled with stories of great men and women who embodied this principle. For instance, we read of Moses going up Mount Sinai alone to contemplate and pray. We read of Mohammed, peace be upon him, retreating to the Cave of Hira for quiet prayer and contemplation. We read of St. Mary of Egypt withdrawing into the Jordanian desert for self-reflection. We read of Jesus Christ spending forty days in the Judean desert, fasting and getting ready for the start of his mission. These figures understood the relevance of self-awareness and its connection to growing their divine missions. How else could we grow if we do not spend quality time reflecting on our identity and purpose?

A life that is not scrutinized is not worth living.

This scrutiny involves being brutally honest with our strengths and weaknesses. Identifying our weaknesses can be painful, but is it worth the discomfort? Absolutely.

A baby cries when it is born because it is used to the comfort and stability of the womb. Are its cries of discomfort worth it? Of course.

Migrating to the United States can involve long and tedious paperwork, research, screenings and waiting. Is the tedious process worth it? Some of you would agree it is.

Parents are sometimes in tears when they drop their kids in college or walk them down the aisle. Is the transition pain worth it? You can bet on it.

A lot of you have spent long hours and sleepless nights doing homework, completing research papers and getting ready for exams. Is the certificate worth the sleepless nights? Without question.

In the same way, the pain associated with growth must not deter you. Its fruits far outweigh any torment the process presents. Beware your comfort zone, it is a dreadful state that has stunted the growth of so many. Do not let it stunt yours. The most important step in reversing a relapse to our comfort zones is truly knowing who we are.

Albert Einstein, with all his incredible contributions to physics, loved to play the violin and sing. Did he ever become as good as Mozart?

Barack Obama, with his eloquence and leadership prowess, could decide to take African fiction classes. Could he ever surpass Chimamanda Adichie's ingenuity in that field?

Bill Gates, with his gifted business and computing acumen, loves playing tennis during his spare time. Could he ever defeat

Serena Williams on a court?

The reverse arguments could be made about Mozart, Chimamanda or Serena. Of course they could learn physics, public speaking, leadership and computer science, but could they achieve the same heights of greatness as Albert, Barack or Bill? Probably not with the same ease.

The point here is to underscore the importance of knowing yourself and making a conscious effort to grow along the lines of your strengths. That said, once you have identified your strengths, it is time for the painful part of identifying your weaknesses. Thankfully, there is a method and science to helping you flip these weaknesses into strengths. It is summarized as follows:

Once a weakness is identified and thoroughly examined, your brain and will-power automatically turn the weakness into growth triggers.

Many immigrants do not think like victims. We think like survivors. Our brains process disadvantages by seeking solutions—not wallowing in self-pity. While this is not unique to immigrants at all, it is the prevailing mindset among those I have interacted with. I have tried to find a rational explanation for this disposition.

Besides our culture, the closest scientific hypothesis I came up with is a primitive defense system called the limbic system. This system is located in our brains and is permanently alert. It is constantly working whether we are paying attention or not. It feeds off our emotions and triggers a response before we even have time to think about it. It is responsible for making us jump out of the road when we see a car approaching suddenly and it works at a much faster speed than our thoughts. The billion dollar commercial industry takes advantage of this speed by registering their products into our subconscious using short ads. I believe this same system is responsible for subconsciously translating our concerns over our weaknesses into growth triggers. Whether this is scientifically valid or not is not within the scope of this book. However, it is important to remember that:

Once a weakness is identified and thoroughly examined, your brain and will-power automatically turn the weakness into growth triggers.

I'll give personal examples and hopefully they will drive you to identify yours.

I was aware of my communication insecurity. People would ask me to either repeat myself or speak a little louder. This hurt my confidence a lot. However, this painful awareness also automatically inspired a growth trigger. I began googling at least ten words every day. Not their definitions, but their pronunciations in American English. From Google, I started using YouTube so that I could hear these pronunciations as used by different subscribers.

Some days, I did not make it to ten new words, other days I went beyond ten, and yet, on other days, I did not search for any words. However, acknowledging this limitation kept me on my toes and helped me overcome the insecurity.

On my bus rides back from work, I would sometimes ask the person sitting next to me how they pronounced certain words. This turned out to be a good conversation starter. I met Andrea, Steve and a few others this way. They taught me how to properly pronounce several words. For instance, Steve stressed that "either" was not pronounced as "EYE-ther" and, despite my doubts about it, he was certain that "route" was not pronounced as "root".

Andrea, on the other hand, made it clear that "tomato" was actually "tuh-MAY-toe" and that "Finna" was a legitimate blend of "fixing" and "to".

I never really argued with them—except playfully. And when they would drop off on their exits, I recited those words again and again until they stuck.

I also learned to talk slower. I realized that people understood me better when I pronounced every syllable of each word. To do that, I needed to slow down and Americanize the ring of each word. These practices were effective. At work, my customers and coworkers stopped asking me to repeat myself or speak louder. It was such a relief that they could understand me in one take. However, to achieve this important communication feat, I had to acknowledge my weakness and, in the process, this birthed the structured growth trigger. Again:

Once a weakness is identified and thoroughly examined, your brain and will-power automatically turn the weakness into growth triggers.

Another example was my gradual consciousness of my cowardice with confronting authority. It's hard to accept that one is a coward but I was one and, thankfully, I came to that realization. Otherwise, I would still remain one today. I couldn't express my concerns to managers or people in authority—even when it was important for solving work problems.

This spinelessness was especially glaring when contrasted with my African American coworkers. Their boldness was both shocking and attractive. They expressed themselves in ways that I could not, but which I wished that I could. I started to realize that we were more different than I had imagined. Despite sharing the same skin color, we saw and expressed ourselves differently.

It dawned on me that I did not share their history of slavery or civil rights activism, and they did not share my culture of excessive reverence for superiors or leaders. They were fearless and spoke their minds to authority. I was raised in a culture where we learned by observation—not by asking questions. A culture where questioning authority could be suicidal and where people become successful by being friendly and courteous with those they did not necessarily like. This form of hypocrisy had almost become second nature to me—more like a survival instinct. I had been wired to smile at unfair bosses as long as I kept my job. Having said that, this hypocrisy and cowardice was stifling. I did not voice my opinion even if it helped the group or made my job easier.

I was also very uncomfortable with saying "no".

This meant that I started taking on tasks I shouldn't have taken on, because I did not want to appear disrespectful. Despite my self-confidence, servant leadership and time management, I was in many ways a doormat. In my mind, saying no meant I was lazy and incompetent. It was also a sign of disrespect. So, I said yes to nearly all requests and this negatively impacted my productivity. Having said that, this self-awareness lead to a growth trigger. I started practicing different ways of saying no without being rude. I learned to do this by providing the reasons why I could not take on their requests.

I started to use sentences like:

'I would love to do this, however, I need ...'

'I can absolutely help with this if ...'

'I completely understand the importance of this task. Could you send me something in writing so ...?'

These sentences helped me fuse the American culture of

outspokenness with my culture of respect. I had successfully turned my cowardice and hypocrisy into strengths. This is yet another example of the truth that:

Once a weakness is identified and thoroughly examined, your brain and will-power automatically turn the weakness into growth triggers.

I was also acutely aware of my distaste for change. I was a creature of habit and still am. I park in the same parking spot, buy coffee from the same Dunkin Donut location and I scarcely let a week go without driving to the same Chipotle. Nevertheless, here I was in a corporation where change was a certainty. Every month, there was a new bit of training, a new technological upgrade and new customer demands. I realized that the stability I craved was a pipe dream. However, as with other weaknesses, acknowledging this helped initiate a growth trigger for me.

As I thoroughly examined this weakness, it hit me that whenever I understood the reasons behind a change, I was prone to support it. Taking a few hours to research and question why our processes were always changing became my weapon against this weakness.

It actually helped me predict change before it happened. I found myself helping coworkers deal with change and put it in the right perspective. I would talk about the benefits of the new technological tools and what they could help us achieve. I would tell them about the security gaps of the old tools and how a certain company got compromised and lost millions of dollars using those tools. They began to see why we were adopting the new tools or the new processes.

This growth would not have been possible if I did not know and acknowledge my shortcomings when it comes to change.

Again:

Once a weakness is identified and thoroughly examined, your brain and will-power automatically turn the weakness into growth triggers.

Furthermore, I knew I was a poor visual learner. I had poor retention if I did not take notes. Typing on a computer did not substitute for this lack. The same was true about setting up calendar reminders. If I did not put an activity on my calendar or scribble it down on my scratchpad, it would likely slip my attention. My acknowledgement of my poor attention span became a growth trigger. Everywhere I go—even to this very day—I carry a pen and a scratchpad, or sticky notes.

Once a weakness is identified and thoroughly examined, your brain and will-power automatically turn the weakness into growth triggers.

By the same token, I knew I could not make good jokes with my customers because of my limited exposure to American culture. For instance, customers and coworkers called me "Obi wan Kenobi". They would typically marvel at the thought that I had never watched the Star Wars movie. Their jokes were lost on me. This and many other mainstays of the American culture helped me refine and structure my conversations. I kept them restricted to topics such as the weather.

I also learned to use phrases like, "I know, right?" Or even just, "Right!"

These words kept my customers talking while I executed the work at hand.

Again:

Once a weakness is identified and thoroughly examined, your brain and will-power automatically turn the weakness into growth triggers.

I could go on and on about the relevance of self-awareness and its link to structured growth. However, I think you get the message. At least, the ancient Greeks did. This is why a 2500-year-old Greek inscription in Apollo's temple reads:

"γνῶθι σεαυτόν"

This loosely translates to:

"Know thyself"

Without knowing yourself, you cannot improve yourself. You cannot grow. You blow wherever the wind blows. You run because others are running. You climb because others are climbing.

You should expect to fall when others are falling.

This is because you do things because others are doing it and not because you see any intrinsic value in it. As stated in the introduction of this book, the opposite of success is conformity with society without knowing why, or knowing yourself. Upon knowing yourself, you will realize how much power and control you have over yourself and over the changes in your environment.

Change is inevitable in corporate America as well as in real life. The real question is, how do you prepare for it? How do you position yourself to take advantage of an inevitable occurrence?

If you do not control change, it can control—and potentially destroy—you.

In order to better control changes at work, I was convinced I needed to go back to school. I knew a degree would open doors and make me more relevant at work. However, I also wanted to make sure that the degree I chose would be worth the investment.

This was harder than I thought.

After months of research, I decided to go for a degree in Management and Information Systems. I chose that field because of my job at the time and because of its wide applicability to the American job market. Technology and people are some of the biggest drivers of change in corporate America. I felt that mastering both would put me in a good position to navigate the turbulent waves of change. I did my research and, once convinced, I went for it. Thankfully, my employer—as many employers in corporate America do—offered a tuition reimbursement package.

I am compelled to state here that this does not mean you cannot enjoy success in other fields. However, I encourage you, if unsure about what to go for, to think long and hard about the STEM fields (Science, Technology, Engineering & Math). This is because college in America is very much a business. It is therefore logical to aspire for a return on that investment. However, this suggestion must not overrule your discernment and self-evaluation results. Ergo, know yourself.

The next thing I did was search for the least expensive, yet accredited, university that offered that program. I narrowed my options down to the Metropolitan State University in Minneapolis. With the tuition reimbursement program and reduced cost of education, I graduated with minimal student loans.

Homework was not fun, but I learned a lot. For instance, I developed a mastery for visual tools such as Visio and UML modelling. I learned how to present problems succinctly using these tools. Even before graduating, I started applying this knowledge at work and my employer started treating me as if I already had the master's degree. They would often ask me to take on tasks beyond my position or have me make presentations to clients.

These extra responsibilities boosted my self-confidence. The feeling of inadequacy was slowly giving way to a self-awareness of my strengths and value.

With the extra responsibilities came raises.

At this point, I bought my first car and took up paying college tuition for my siblings back home. I even considered myself good enough to run for elections at the university senate. I eventually secured enough votes to join the senate and become a voice for change.

The reason I list these achievements is to emphasize the relevance of knowing oneself to personal growth. The timid immigrant who was insecure about his communication skills had become so confident in his abilities that every facet of his life started to positively change. He stopped reacting to life's changes and started architecting those changes.

At the end of the day, being the master of your destiny requires mastering change. To master or control change, structured growth is inevitable and comes down to the following principles and disciplines:

1. Think for yourself (don't conform without knowing why)
2. Identify your strengths
3. Spend quality time identifying your weaknesses
4. Take small steps to counterbalance identified weaknesses (thankfully, you are wired to do so)
5. Don't stay where you are. Keep growing …

And remember:

Once a weakness is identified and thoroughly examined, your brain and will-power automatically turn the weakness into growth triggers.

Transgression of this Principle:

Second century Roman Emperor Commodus defied this principle to epic proportions. He was a megalomaniac, who proclaimed himself to be the reincarnation of the legendary Hercules, and participated in gladiator battles every evening, in which he 'won' every fight. Roman citizens, missing their limbs through accident or illness were taken to the arena, where they were tied together for Commodus to club to death while pretending they were giants. He was also notorious for slaying his gladiator-practice opponents. These gladiator victories angered so many Romans because they knew they were staged and stacked in his favor. His personal delusions extended beyond the arena. In the year 192, he re-founded Rome and changed the name of the eternal city to his name "Colonia Commodiana". He even changed the twelve months of the calendar year to his twelve names (he took on several middle names) and decreed that every Roman citizen take up the last name; Commodianus. Fed up with his theatrics, Commodus was assassinated in December of 192 and the Roman senate restored the original name of the eternal city back to Rome. He is an unfortunate example of a man who did not truly know himself and thus couldn't grow beyond his illusions of grandeur.

The legendary Michael Jordan embodies both an observer and a transgressor of this principle. He is widely regarded as the greatest basketball player of all time and that is thanks to his knowing and growing his rare talent. In other words, he observed this principle for much of his professional career.

However, in February of 1994, Jordan signed a contract with the Chicago White Sox to play baseball. After an abysmal season, he moved to the Arizona fall league where he failed as well. In an interview, Michael called himself the team's "worst player" and gave up professional baseball altogether. Fortunately, Jordan's brief stint as a pro baseball player did not ruin his basketball career or reputation. While he made an erroneous calculation in overestimating his baseball skills, he soon reassessed himself and realized that was not his forte. Upon his return to basketball, he went on to be named MVP two more times and his place in history is still unrivalled. His transgression of the principle of knowing and growing oneself, did not hinder him from eventually observing it and benefitting from its fruits.

Observance of this Principle:

In May of 2019, Frank Baez made the news waves for graduating with a nursing degree in the same institution he started out as a janitor. Leaving his home country of the Dominican Republic at only fifteen, with very little money and poor command of the English language, Frank never gave up. He worked long hours cleaning patient rooms, dirty bathrooms and hallways at the Langone Tisch Hospital in New York. These long hours and the near absence of family or a social life, did not deter him from making the most of himself. After years of cleaning, he applied successfully for a position as a patient transporter. With his new job, he was tasked with taking patients to and from their rooms for surgeries and other lab tests. The new job also afforded him a means to get into college, where he excelled and became the first person in his family to get a college degree. Those years working in the hospital helped him find his passion. He realized that he enjoyed helping the sick and was darn good at it. Frank was well aware of his strengths and leveraged them to get into his career of choice.He is a great example of a migrant who defied the long odds by embodying the principle laid down in this chapter.

Soichiro Honda, the great Japanese engineer who established one of the world's most profitable auto companies – the Honda Motor Company we all know today, is a prime example of the value of knowing and growing oneself. He spent his early childhood helping his father, a blacksmith, with his bicycle repair business and had no interest in traditional or formal education. Despite attempts by his parents to push him into the conventional educational system, Honda was well aware of his strengths and weaknesses and sought to explore his strengths. As a child, he remembers being thrilled at seeing a car drive through his village. It was the first time he had ever seen a car. He said several times that he could never forget the smell of oil that the car gave off. As a teenager, he once borrowed his father's bicycle to see a demonstration of an airplane made by renowned pilot Art Smith. The experience stuck with him and consolidated his love for machinery and invention. At the age of fifteen, without any traditional education, Honda left the comfort of his home to pursue his dreams of being a mechanic in Tokyo. There, as an apprentice, he learned how to fix different vehicles and broadened his general knowledge of cars. He lived very modestly and was able to save up the little money he made. With his savings, he set up his car repair business at the age of 22. His love for machinery and invention led him to focus his energy in those fields of endeavor and the world can only be thankful that he discovered his strengths and leveraged them to great lengths.

CHAPTER 5

Building Meaningful Relationships

"Be courteous to all, but intimate with few, and let those few be well tried before you give them your confidence. True friendship is a plant of slow growth, and must undergo and withstand the shocks of adversity before it is entitled to the appellation."

- George Washington

The principle of building meaningful relationships is intentionally discussed here in Chapter Five. The rationale for this is that we are better poised to develop the healthiest relationships after applying the principles in the previous chapters, such as building confidence and truly knowing ourselves. Only then can we really forge meaningful coalitions that align with our growth goals and vision. "Meaningful" is key here. We touched on this a little bit in Chapter Two. However, while Chapter Two calls for courtesy to all in the spirit of servant leadership, this chapter involves more than courtesy or servant leadership. It entails forging close bonds and building beneficial relationships with a select few.

The Igbos have so many proverbs that capture the importance of choosing one's close company carefully. One of them runs:

"Ukpala gbabara n'ikpo okuko, n'ala ala mmuo."

This translates to:

"The grasshopper that runs into the midst of fowls, will end up in the land of the spirits."

Another one says:

"Oke oshimmiri anokataghi rie onye obula nke o na-ahughi ukwu ya anya."

This translates to:

"The ocean never swallows a person whose leg it does not come in contact with."

Both proverbs shed light on the magnitude of the danger of forging close alliances with people who are not aligned with one's goals.

The right alliances, on the other hand, can unravel opportunities we would otherwise not be privy to. It is important to seize these opportunities and doing this involves developing certain soft skills. Soft skills such as a positive attitude, dependability and empathy, never go out of style. They constitute some of the best investments we can make in our professional careers. Our chances of finding jobs, getting promoted or pursuing business ventures are greatly enhanced by the quality of our professional networks. Just as a well spun spider's web attracts and entraps its prey; a well spun professional network attracts and maximizes our opportunities. However, instead of the sticky silk strands of the spider's web, we leverage commonsense soft skills and sound judgement.

The rise of artificial intelligence and automation in the United States means that many people who rely solely on hard skills may gradually get replaced by automated systems. However, those who have honed the art of collaboration, positive attitude, persuasion, people management and other relationship-building skills could stay relevant. Furthermore, the "command-and-control" model we are used to in many African work cultures will prove problematic in the current American corporate system which is gradually moving towards a more inclusive and engaging culture. It is therefore important to work on developing our soft skills, as they not only accentuate our professional relevance, but are critical with building strong relationships.

These soft skills, combined with a mastery of the principles laid down in the earlier chapters are pivotal to creating and seizing meaningful opportunities. Otherwise, we could be exposed to unhelpful relationships that do not further our personal or professional goals. One of such relationships—albeit personal—was the one I had with Deborah. She was one of the more beautiful ladies I worked with at my first job in the US. She stood at about five-four, attractive, with penetrating gray eyes and a heart palpitating smile. Her curly hair hung down past her shoulders, like the dolls my sisters grew up playing with. She playfully curled strands of her hair around and around her fingers. Somehow, she managed to wear a no-nonsense look on her face which melted away when we locked eyes. She would quickly look away and then continue playing with her hair, fully aware I was watching her. And while I may have been naïve to the US culture, the language of flirtation is universal.

I could not bring myself to approach her. I was still insecure and dealing with the culture shock of the new environment. The most I ever did was wave back or smile and then chastise myself afterwards. "Obi, you're a coward" I would say to myself. But the following day, I would do the exact same thing; smile and watch her play with her hair. After about a week or two of foolish flirting, she took the initiative and introduced herself.

"Hi, I'm Deborah. I see you all the time."

"Hi, I'm Obi."

"Obi? Like Obi Wan Kenobi? That's such a cool name," she said.

"Thank you. Deborah is a cool name, too."

"Thank you. I'm glad you didn't try to call me Debby. I hate when people do that. Don't you hate it when they screw up your name?"

"I know right"

We exchanged numbers and that was it. My first American girlfriend. The first two weeks were the stuff of romantic movies. Movie dates, walking in the picturesque snow and endless text messaging. However, by the end of the second week, I learned about her children. She had three of them. I was surprised because I had been to her house and hadn't seen any children or even pictures of children.

"We just moved in there Obi. And they were with their dads for that weekend," she explained.

"Dads?"

"Yes. I've been burned one too many times. But I'm strong now. I keep a cordial relationship with their fathers. Hope you don't have a problem with that?"

"No. Not at all."

"You sure? You don't look too happy."

"Yea. It's not a problem," I lied.

The realization of the three children from different fathers deflated me. It haunted me every night I went to sleep on Ike's couch. I wondered what my family would think, whether I was prepared to deal with the situation in the long run, and how to broach my internal conflicts, about it all, with her. I was too afraid to speak up and lose her, and at the same time, too timid to challenge my cultural bias. I had yet to evolve into the confident man who knew himself and was capable of saying no or making the right decision. As days turned into weeks, the rigid dichotomy between my emotional and cultural lenses grew. I had to find a way to control this.

We both wanted to grow within the company and understood that dating publicly could prove problematic. So we agreed to keep our relationship quiet. However, only a few weeks later, it seemed like everyone knew about us. Jamil, the security guard at the desk once smiled at me while Deborah was walking by.

"I hear you're hitting that," he said with a mischievous wink.

I could not believe what I heard—or saw.

"What?" I asked in terror. "Hitting what?"

"Yeah, I see you, bro. She ain't bad at all," Jamil continued with a sinister smile. "She looks good, bro."

"Who told you that?"

"Shii ... she's telling everyone, bro. These females can't keep quiet. Did you think she would be quiet?" He chuckled.

"She told other people?"

"Yup. Everybody knows, bro. The whole call center and their families and friends."

"You're funny," I replied, feigning a smile as I walked away.

It wasn't funny. I needed to stop this right in its tracks. I did not come to America to become the stuff of office gossip.

The same evening, I confronted her and she flat out denied telling anyone.

"I swear I didn't tell anybody. Nobody knows, Obi."

I knew she was not being truthful.

"Are you sure?" I asked again.

"Yes, Obi. Are you calling me a liar?"

"No, I'm not."

"Yes, you are …"

I decided not to push any further. The conversation had become tense. I could see a rush of emotions sending color to her cheeks and flooding her eyes. So I changed the topic and asked how her kids were doing.

About a week later, while seated in a town hall with the HR manager and a group of employees, I kept mulling over my relationship status. Whenever anyone smiled at me, I automatically assumed it had something to do with me and Deborah. It was quickly becoming paranoia. The HR lady was talking about the importance of avoiding counterproductive workplace behaviors. There had been an uptick in reports that employees were clocking in and out for their peers. She attributed this to the practice of sharing passwords among employees – especially between those in personal relationships.

"Timecard fraud is a felony under Penal Code section 424," she said before going on to discuss best practices with respect to romance and dating at work.

"You need to disclose it if you are, so that you are not on the same teams and there is no conflict of interest…"

After work that day, Deborah and I talked about the details of the town hall meeting. Even though we never exchanged passwords, I explained my fear that our relationship could stifle my ability to grow within the company.

"I have a family in Africa depending on me, Deb. I cannot take care of them with ten dollars an hour. We need to figure something out cos these people will not promote either of us if they found out we were dating."

"That's not true," she shot back, without adding any evidence to support her argument.

"You know it is Deb, and besides, you haven't stopped talking. Yesterday, Jeremy told me you told him we were an item."

"An item?"

"Yes. You know, like boyfriend and girlfriend."

"I never use that word."

"That's not the point, Deb. I keep hearing these things from so many people even after we agreed not to talk to anyone."

"Jeremy is sick."

"Is Patrick sick, too?"

"Obi, those guys have been bugging me. What do you want me to tell them? You want me to say I'm single? They are sick and the only way to stop 'em is to tell him about you. About us."

"Are the girls sick, too?"

"I didn't tell the girls. I promise. They must have heard me talking to Jeremy. Or maybe he told them. You know he likes to talk like a bitch. I can't believe you're …And why does it bother you if the girls know? Are you trying to get with them?"

"I'm done with this, Deb. I'm over it."

"You're breaking up with me?"

"Yes, Deb. It's over."

"Wow! Just like that? Wow! I see how it is. You want those nasty, fake girls at work. I see how it is. Go get them and I hope you get what's coming for you. I hope you catch an STD..."

She was distraught, but I stuck with my decision.

It is important to point out that this situation could have been averted or handled differently if I had applied the principles discussed in the prior chapters. It is cowardly to deceptively awaken the emotions of anyone—woman or man—with no intentions of loving them through thick and thin. Some of us do this because we are afraid we will not find someone else to love us, i.e. the fear of missing out. True self-knowledge (Chapter Four) eliminates this fear factor. Some of us do this because we lack confidence in ourselves and our worth. The principle of self-esteem (Chapter Three), helps counteract this inclination. Some of us do this for purely selfish reasons. We end up forging faux relationships with multiple people and disappointing all or some of them. The principle of servant leadership (Chapter Two) dispels this self-centered mindset by helping us put tremendous value on other people's time and interests (Chapter One).

As you can see, it is crucial to internalize the principles laid down in the previous chapters before forging close relationships, especially personal ones, at work.

There is an old adage that goes, "Never get your honey where you make your money". The value of this adage is extraordinary. However, this does not mean that you cannot find love at your place of employment or that your work relationship is destined to fail.

As migrants, many of us are brought up to question the long-term play of almost everything. Our parents push us to study courses or majors that improve our long-term prosperity and prestige after college. Our families often go into extensive research on the families we marry into, to strengthen and accentuate long-term partnerships. Our societies encourage us to bear multiple children as insurance against poverty during our old age. As ugly and pressure-packed these practices and traditions can be, they inadvertently instill a long-term mindset in us. Our cars, our purchases, our employment opportunities, our promotions and even our relationships are better evaluated through the prism of plausible long-term goals. If you decide to get into a romantic relationship at work, it is important to assess such a relationship through the same cultural lens. Is it likely to end up as a brief affair or could it lead to a long-term partnership, such as a marriage? The latter scenario, in my opinion, is the one worth giving a shot if you decide to forge romantic relationships at work. As old-fashioned as this sounds, we come from cultures that encourage these long-term perspectives.

When sex and romance get involved, emotions often do. And these emotions, like volcanic eruptions, do erupt—and often with disastrous consequences. I have seen people who were in love slash each other's tires. I have heard about court cases, restraining orders, divorces, demotions and full-blown physical fights.

It typically ends ugly.

On the other hand, there are ample stories of loose talk, uncomfortable winks, nasty innuendos and outright flirting. I know an immigrant lady who has been called *exotic* more than a few times—as if it were a compliment. These experiences can be uncomfortable and constitute counterproductive workplace behaviors.

The presence of a power dynamic further muddies the waters of workplace romance or flirtation. For instance, how do you know if your attraction to your manager has more to do with their position and less to do with his or her personal charm? And if you were the manager in question. How do you truly tell if your subordinate is with you because they are attracted to you or to your position? How do you hold them accountable for work gaps and stay enamored to them? How do you create an impression of impartiality, which all leaders ought to have? How do you handle the fallout of a breakup or an abuse-of-power litigation? This is why several companies institute anti-fraternization policies.

These policies do not necessarily deter certain people from indulging in workplace romance or making sexual advances. In other words, expect these things to happen and prepare for it!

It takes one who is secure about themselves to turn down sexual advances and still maintain a cordial friendship with the flirter. This balance is important—but tricky for some of us who may crave validation or acceptance in our new society. Moving from a communal society to an individualistic one comes with a feeling of isolation and loneliness. Back home, we could turn to family and friends for support. Here, it's easy to feel all alone. It is no wonder we typically crave the communal experience and inter-dependence we enjoyed in the motherland. We are eager to make and keep friends to compensate for this feeling of isolation. This compensation mechanism can drive us to say yes to relationships that could hurt us. If interactions and advances becomes uncomfortable, speak to someone in authority such as your human resources manager. Your workplace should not be an uncomfortable space. It is also crucial to restate here the value of internalizing the principles discussed in earlier chapters. When this is done, solid relationships are more likely than not.

Carolyn exemplified the solid relationship alluded to earlier. She was the business director for one of the clients we did business with. In other words, she was the ultimate arbiter on whether my company kept their business or not. She was revered and feared by the management of my company. Revered because she was knowledgeable and great at what she did. Feared because she could sniff out bullshit from a mile away. And if she did not like the direction of things, she could withdraw her business at a moment's notice.

Now and again, the business directors of the companies we worked for would visit our office, observing our processes. Most were content with an office space away from the production floor. But Carolyn loved to see the 'action'. She loved to listen to how our employees were handling customers' issues and what questions they had. To ensure we made a good impression, my manager gave her visibility to my team. He would set up a workstation for her right next to mine. I took this as a compliment because they trusted that my team and I would make a good impression on Carolyn. Furthermore, the optics of a black man in charge of a high performing team were good for my company.

"Obi is almost done with his master's degree," my manager said to Carolyn. "And he is taking advantage of our tuition reimbursement program. Smart guy"

"That's awesome"

She was aware of this, but for some reason he repeated it more than once—maybe to drive home the impression that my company was a beacon for diversity and inclusion.

Carolyn and I became friends. Our conversations were sometimes intense, but we never crossed the professional line. She criticized things she believed we were doing wrong, while

I poked holes in some of her propositions. She had successfully created an atmosphere where I could speak my mind without fear of retribution and I could tell she appreciated my honesty. We respected each other and that working relationship was refreshing.

When she had lunches with my superiors and directors, she would usually request that I tag along. I was flattered to know she thought so highly of me.

One morning, on one of her visits, Carolyn told me she was bringing new business for us.

"Obi, I would want you to own it," she said. "It's a great opportunity for your company and they just approved the statement of work"

"That sounds good. What do you mean own it?"

"I mean I want you in charge of it. I want to start with twenty agents and if they do well—if *you* do well—we may grow it to three hundred and you guys may need to get another building."

"That would be awesome. Tell me more about it," I prodded.

She explained some more about the potential of the new line of business and how much value it could bring to my company and to hers'. She also elaborated on the similarities between my current role and the efforts involved in running the new contract.

I was thrilled and I remember being unable to sleep that night. The thought of being in charge of an important contract—not just a team of agents—was mind blowing.

The business eventually came. And, true to her words, Carolyn lobbied with my company to put me in charge. However, my company—in a bid to save costs—did not give me any monetary compensation or promotion to go with the new responsibility. I did the work, but received the same pay. Their reasons varied. One director said it was still a small business and did not require that much oversight from me. This turned out to be untrue as I worked long hours and even weekends to meet our commitments to Carolyn's company. Another director said it was the end of the fiscal year and they could not make such monetary changes at the time. Whatever their reasons, they we all unanimous in urging me to be patient. They assured me that in due time I would get the accompanying title and monetary benefits.

I carried on executing my duties with as cheerful an attitude as I could muster and to the best of my abilities. However, despite the new fiscal year and growth in the business from twenty to almost sixty agents, I did not get the promotion or salary bump. This hurt me and I felt betrayed by an organization I had trusted with all my heart. This highlights the reality of corporate America. Like most capitalist systems, profits sometimes take precedence over promises made to employees.

I had developed an intense loyalty to my employer, largely because they were the first company I worked for in the United States and had been footing a large portion of my tuition. This loyalty also meant that I could not tell Carolyn that, despite her kind words, I was really not getting paid what I deserved. It was tough deciding what the right thing to do was.

So I started applying to other jobs. And soon enough, I got invited to a few interviews. One of the companies I interviewed for made me an offer. It was for twenty thousand dollars more than I was earning at the time. I was thrilled, but afraid of leaving a company I had been with for so long. After much thought, I brought the offer letter to my manager and to one of the directors.

I told them that while I loved working for them, I was getting underpaid for the work I did. I explained how my duties went beyond that of a regular team lead and then presented them the paperwork containing the offer I had just received. I told them that I would stay if they paid me even five thousand dollars less than the new employer was willing to pay. However, if they were not inclined to do so, I would have to accept the other offer.

"Are you quitting?" my manager asked

"Not if you're going to offer me the business manager role and the compensation," I responded

"We will get back to you on that, however, we will be accepting this as your two-week notice. I'll have the HR manager set up an exit interview."

"Okay. I appreciate it"

This stung me. I expected them to show a little more effort in trying to keep me. How could they easily cut me off? It was a sad moment but it reaffirmed that I made the right choice in looking for another job.

A few days later, Carolyn was at the office. She had not been on the production floor, but locked in a meeting with my company's management. While she was leaving, she stopped at my desk to check on me and say goodbye. It was then that I told her that I had given my two-week notice the previous week. The next Thursday would be my last day at work.

She looked like she was going to have a heart-attack.

"What?"

"Yea"

"Obi, can we talk about this? Can I talk to you about this?"

"Of course."

"Is now a good time?"

"Yes"

"El-Loro?"

"Yes. Thank you."

She insisted on buying dinner at the Mexican restaurant next to the office. After ordering food, she asked why I was leaving.

I told her everything: how I had taken on the new business and worked diligently to make it successful. How I was promised a promotion and a new job title, but still had the title and salary of a team leader.

Carolyn turned pale. She adjusted her seat and tucked away the stray strands of blond hair in her eyes. I could see how inflamed they were. I had never seen her look so angry.

"What?" she exclaimed. "You have not gotten a raise since last July?"

"No, ma'am. Same money. Same title. And I was willing to—"

"Obi, would you stay if they increased your pay?" she cut in.

"Yes, I would. I love working with you and your company. And, honestly, I don't know a lot about the culture of the new company. A part of me is worried that it may not be as good as..."

"Say no more," Carolyn interjected again. "Could you give me a day or two?"

I nodded as she scribbled notes on her notepad.

Our burritos arrived and the rest of the dinner was spent writing down the pros and cons of staying with my current employer. When we were done, she paid and handed me the paper on which she scribbled down the pros and cons. I thanked her and we exited El Loro.

The next evening, my manager invited me to his office. He had an offer letter on the table.

"Congratulations Obi!"

"Thank you sir."

It was five thousand dollars less than the offer from the other company. In hindsight, I could have bargained for more. But I was mentally exhausted at this point and decided to sign the offer. Besides, it was fifteen thousand dollars more than my salary at the time.

This story demonstrates one of the many benefits of forging meaningful relationships. My professional relationship with Carolyn opened doors that would have taken much longer to open. I am convinced that this was possible, thanks to my internalization of the principles laid down in the preceding chapters.

One important trait in the art of building meaningful relationships is an acute awareness of non-verbal cues. There are hidden meanings behind facial expressions, eye contact, shrugs, posture and even tone of voice. Body language can tell you more about people than what they say. Even when they are silent, they are still saying something. It is important to pay attention to these.

The communal culture in most African societies ought to give us some edge with these non-verbal cues. From our early childhoods, we are exposed to a wide range of mannerisms. We are flooded with relatives, acquaintances and friends, who become practically family. We learn to communicate with different people in specific ways that reflect their communication needs. And we are familiar with the direct reprimands they mete out if, for instance, we do not greet them properly or ask how they are doing. This community of people subconsciously teach us, from a young age, to read and appreciate body language.

This comes in handy in building affiliations in corporate America and beyond. You are sensitive to others' dispositions, and can more easily decide on the appropriateness of, the subject, the medium, and especially the audience of certain conversations. A personal reprimand, for instance, is usually better in a personal, one-on-one, setting so that its constructiveness is not wasted. Making such a reprimand in a public email chain—which happens often in corporate America—leads to animosity, tension and strife.

While the average African migrant may have mastered the skill of reading non-verbal cues, many of us do a poor job in controlling our non-verbal communication. It is one thing to be aware of others' unspoken words, it's another to be conscious of ours. Things like a weak handshake, sarcasm-soaked voice, speedy words, smirking, subtle hand movements and an unsteady gaze may communicate things you don't mean to.

Stress and worry can compromise your emotional equilibrium and, in so doing, affect your unspoken communication. It can also distort your perception of others' moods and intentions. It is important to be conscious of this, and to eliminate, or at least minimize unnecessary stress. Forming and nurturing good habits such as consistent exercise and meditation, getting rid of toxic friendships or relationships and getting quality sleep—are all helpful ways of dealing with this.

Another non-verbal behavior that puts people off, is micromanaging. It is the ultimate demotivating attitude. In spite of overwhelming research-based evidence on the ills of this management style, and companies encouraging their managers to move away from it, it is still prevalent. There may be isolated cases where this management style is called for but, overall, it is one of the biggest drivers of attrition and dissatisfaction in many organizations. Constantly checking and looking for progress may seem intuitive, but it can come across as being controlling and having no trust in the employee's skills.

This, understandably, would put off the average person, especially in individualistic cultures where independence and autonomy are prized. In more communal cultures, people are a little more tolerant of micromanagement. If you worked for some time in West Africa before moving to the West, you may not find micromanaging as stifling as the average American does. You are used to managers who are domineering, bossy and know-it-all. However, this also means that, all things being equal, you are likely to get on much better with the micromanaging American bosses you work for than some of your co-workers will. Ironically, this could be an advantage for you.

Some tell-tale signs of micromanagers include a reluctance to delegate their duties, a habit of constantly checking on their team, a perception of themselves as the only ones with good ideas and an overwhelming disgust for them from most members of their teams. Do not fall into the trap of being disgusted by such managers. Many of them are subject-matter experts with poor leadership skills. It is easy to join the bandwagon in condemning them, but then you miss out on the wealth of knowledge and skills they could impart on you. In my experience, forging professional relationships—such as mentoring—with such managers has been beneficial. Irrespective of where you are in your career, having the right mentor—albeit a micromanager—can accelerate your growth in corporate America. You do not need to go at it alone, especially when others have charted the path you intend to go. Let go of your ego and fears. Set up an appointment or walk up to someone today and ask if they could mentor you!

Another important aspect of the principle of meaningful relationships is the quality of the company you keep at work. For instance, if you keep having lunch with coworkers who indulge in office gossip or idle talk, you lose the power conferred by this principle. If your inner circle comprises of negative people who keep complaining and whining, you put yourself at a disadvantage. Their negativity will eventually rub off you.

No matter how good you are, if you surround yourself with the wrong people, the benefits of the principles discussed in the previous chapters are eroded. You can manage your time flawlessly, become the best servant leader, build your self-confidence and even grow your skills. However, all those gains are quickly nullified by consistently hanging with the wrong crowd. History and literature are filled with great people who were negatively impacted by their inner circle. The great Julius Caesar was betrayed and executed by his close friend, Brutus. Thomas Sankara of Burkina Faso too, was double-crossed and eventually murdered by his closest associate, Blaise Compaoré. The same can be said of the herculean figure, Samson, and how his lover, Delilah, destroyed him. In Shakespeare's tragedy, we see how King Duncan is murdered by his cousin, Macbeth. And who could forget the treachery of Judas Iscariot and that sickening kiss of death? The list is endless. There is no question that the quality of people we let into our inner circles can hurt us. Be very picky!

Being picky requires setting up boundaries. These boundaries could also apply to family. One of the biggest hurdles that migrants face is taking care of their families back home. It is commonplace to support sick cousins, aging parents and grandparents, as well as unemployed relatives. This is a worthy tradition, but it can also become an impediment to growth. It can be burdensome, especially with the perception that living in America automatically makes one rich. I know immigrants who have taken on loans and extra jobs to take care of relatives back home. This sort of family dynamic can lead to undue stress and strife, and must be managed. It is okay to say no sometimes. Saying yes will not endear you to everyone either—there will always be criticism about your support not being adequate or frequent enough—so focus your energy on relationships that advance your physical, professional and mental wellbeing. This is not to say that you break the tradition of supporting your family. They may need your help and deserve your support. However, your assistance must be commensurate to your earnings and should not rob you of sleep and peace, nor deter your goals.

Furthermore, the principle of building meaningful relationships isn't complete without giving careful consideration to social media. It is a legitimate tool for forging relationships, and at the same time, it has led to the destruction of many relationships. I know people who have lost their jobs for what they posted on Twitter or Facebook. I know employers who routinely scrutinize their employees' social media posts. While it is okay to add and follow friends and coworkers, it is important that you be selective with what you put out there. Take some time to study the privacy policies and settings of the sites you enroll in to ensure that you only have the right audience privy to your personal life. On the other hand, creating a LinkedIn profile is strongly encouraged. Irrespective of your field of endeavor, it is a great way to connect with professionals in your field of interest—even though you are not personally acquainted with them. And even if you decide not to connect with them, you can view their profiles and mirror yours to match theirs. You can see what skills, education, volunteering activities and certifications they have. These can help steer you in the direction you need to go to be just like them—or even better.

I would be remiss to conclude this chapter without paying special attention to the importance of attending professional job conferences and volunteering your time to causes that interest you. These two practices will open more professional doors for you than a thousand job applications would. Conferences like the Society of Women Engineers (SWE) and National Society of Black Engineers (NSBE) are popular yearly events that attract a great deal of corporate giants. These corporations meet one-on-one with attendees and present a goldmine for relationship building. Unfortunately, many people see such conferences as exclusionary or too expensive. However, the seemingly narrow targets of these conferences should not deter anyone. I registered for the SWE conference even though I was not an engineer, nor a woman. It is all about the opportunity to interact with top companies face-to-face. As long as you have paid to attend, you are unlikely to be turned away. The value of these conferences lies in the human touch which you do not get from online applications—which mostly rely on complex algorithms and computer operations. In these conferences, you get an opportunity to forge relationships with people who make hiring decisions and impress them. You will also build relationships with other job seekers which—in my experience—have been equally as helpful. I share this advice—not to endorse any particular conference body—but because it has worked for me and for friends. If you are wary of the cost of attendance, do not hesitate to look for free job conferences. However, in my opinion, the paid options offer greater opportunities.

In conclusion, be friendly to everyone you come across, but be friends with few. This can be tricky, but it is crucial that you master this subtlety. Fusing your communal cultural intelligence with deliberate, professional partnerships can help you overcome the toughest challenges in corporate America. Your network is one of your most valuable assets. It is more important than an impressive resume and can open doors that your skills alone cannot open. The relationships you forge can either take you to new heights or stagnate you. It all comes down to the application of certain disciplines, summarized as follows:

1. Be friendly to all, but friends with a select few
2. Manage relationship boundaries at work, especially when it comes to intimacy.
3. Evaluate the long-term picture while delving into any relationship.
4. Look out for yourself—nobody else will. This is not Africa where your people or community will look out for you.
5. Be aware of all unspoken communication—by others and by yourself. They are much more important than words.
6. Work on reducing stress as it can distort your perception of the intentions of those around you.
7. Be careful about the use of social media.
8. Leverage LinkedIn, professional conferences and other volunteering opportunities.

Transgression of this principle:

In 1939, Vidkung Quisling, the leader of the opposition party in Norway and former minister of defense, was dissatisfied with the declining prominence of his party. So he turned to

Hitler and proposed that Germany help him launch a coup against the Norwegian government at the time. In exchange for Hitler's help, he would help Germany to set up naval bases in Norway. Vidkung also agreed to share national secrets from his time as minister of defense. Hitler loved the idea and gave him his blessings. In April of 1940, Hitler's troops invaded Norway and ousted the legitimate government. However the ousted government fled before they could be captured, leading to the existence of two governments: the legitimate one (on the run) and Vidkung's. In order to legitimize his government, Vidkung asked the Germans for another favor. He asked that they force King Haakon of Norway to declare him the 'head of the government'. However, the Germans were unable to persuade the good king to compromise. Haakon relinquished his throne rather than validate Vidkung Quisling. With little to no popular support, Vidkung soon became useless to Hitler, who sidelined him. Vidkung cut a frustrated figure and lost the respect of his followers. He infamously ordered the execution of police chief Gunnar Eilifsen when the officer refused to arrest five girls who did not show up for forced labor. At home, the resistance to Vidkung continued to increase. And abroad, Germany was losing the war. Vidkung was eventually overthrown, charged for conspiring with Hitler (among other charges) and executed by the firing squad in October of 1945. He is a prime example of the dangers of forging close relationships with the wrong people and his name will always be synonymous with the word 'traitor'. In contrast, the good King Haakon and the noble police chief Eilifsen will be remembered for being brave leaders, who valued the wellbeing of their subjects above their lives and positions of authority.

In 2012, twenty-three year old Aaron Hernandez had become a bona fide National Football League (NFL) superstar.

After a childhood mired by poverty, he had overcome the odds and landed a mouth-watering forty million dollar contract extension with one of the greatest franchises in NFL history. Aaron was living the dream and had helped his family escape the jaws of crippling poverty. He had a beautiful girlfriend who was pregnant with his daughter. However, Aaron was unable to shake off his childhood friends; especially Ernest Wallace and Carlos Ortiz. Despite their bad influence and long criminal rap sheets, Aaron felt some sort of loyalty to them. Months after his contract extension, Aaron was arrested for the 2013 murder of Odin Lloyd. He was eventually convicted in 2015 and sentenced to life behind bars. His friends cut deals with the prosecutors and got very much lighter sentences. Wallace, for instance, got only four and half years as part of his plea deal. In April of 2017, Aaron committed suicide. While Aaron was plagued by other demons and brain trauma, his tragic life underscores the value of being picky about people we bring into our inner circles.

Observance of this principle:

Years before Napoleon Bonaparte became known as 'Napoleon the Great', he was a short, twenty-six year old soldier with the French army. At a dinner party in Paris, he met a thirty-two year old widow named Josephine. Her husband had been executed during the French Revolution. However, Josephine was brilliant, beautiful and caught the young soldier's eye. Against his parents' objections to marrying a widow who was six years older than him, Napoleon soldiered on with the relationship. And as historian Kate Williams explains: "Josephine, the fabulous hostess and skilled diplomat, was the perfect consort to the ambitious but obnoxious Napoleon. With her by his side, he became the greatest man in Europe, the Supreme Emperor…"

There is no question that Josephine was instrumental in helping Napoleon become the great Emperor and historical figure that he became. Their relationship brought out the best in him and helped him shape the landscape of Europe. He was able to navigate the treacherous waters of nineteenth century politics, wars and expeditions. With Josephine by his side, his influence extended beyond politics and the expansive French empire. As a matter of fact, he is credited for the Napoleonic Code which influenced the legal systems of over seventy countries today. Historian Andrew Roberts summarized the impact of his legacy aptly when he wrote: "The ideas that underpin our modern world—meritocracy, equality before the law, property rights, religious toleration, modern secular education, sound finances, and so on—were championed, consolidated, codified and geographically extended by Napoleon." Even though the love between them eventually went cold, he reaped the benefits of her wisdom, counsel and knowledge.

CHAPTER 6
Adding Value

"You do not get paid for the hour. You get paid for the value you bring to the hour."

- Jim Rohn

Once you start growing yourself and building meaningful relationships, you will find that you are in a unique position to start adding value to your workplace. Do not wait to be told to do so. Take the initiative! Starting where you are, there are things you can do to bring value today. This is the greatest guarantor of job security and growth. I know this sounds like one of those annoying clichés, but by the end of this chapter, you will see how you could easily add value to any organization. You will read practical examples that have encyclopedic and scientific applicability. In other words, they can be repeated and applied to almost any work situation to yield similar results. Before exploring those examples, let's try to answer a few questions.

Can you give what you do not have? I think we know the answer to that. Could you show someone how to change a flat tire if you haven't changed one before? Could you teach your neighbor to speak Swahili if you do not speak it yourself? Could you love if you have no love within? Could you add value if you do not value yourself and others? This is why we discuss the principle of "giving value" here. While the preceding chapters have taught us different ways to value ourselves and value others, this chapter discusses adding value to your organization. The argument here is obvious—you cannot do the latter without the former.

In the previous chapter, I was able to add real value to the company only after working on myself and my mindset. I was able to make good visual presentations only after learning how to use the data modeling tools in school. I was able to engage Carolyn in professional conversations and debates only after building up my self-esteem, knowledge and communication skills. I was able to get a promotion only after proving that I brought value to my company.

A big mistake a lot of us make is bringing our needs to our organizations instead of our seeds. The bitter truth is that many societies—especially individualistic ones—do not care about your needs or your lack. They care about your seeds—or what you have to offer.

I remember an interesting coaching session I had with a twenty-one year-old named Nick. He was very intelligent, smart and, despite being one of the youngest agents, he commanded the admiration of his peers. He commanded mine as well. I knew his potential was (and is) great and tried to get him to leverage his strengths.

However, Nick had this nonchalant attitude towards work. He was bored stiff and had lost the fire he had in the first few weeks on the job. And who could blame him? The call center can be monotonous and exceptionally boring. During this coaching session, he was closed off and would not self-identify like he typically would. Unlike our previous sessions, I did more of the talking and my questions were met with one-word replies.

"Your attendance has taken a hit since our last one-on-one.

We couldn't have one last Tuesday cos you weren't in. Is there a reason you have been absent or coming in late so often?" I asked.

"No."

"Is there something happening at home or outside of work that you would like to talk about?"

"Nope," he responded.

"Are you sure? Nothing you would like to share?"

"Nope."

"What about your car? Still working okay?"

"Yup."

"No issues with it?"

"Nope."

"Look, Nick, I care about your success and it's just unlike you to miss so many days and come in late so many times. You know, there's never smoke without fire. Are you sure there is nothing you want to talk about to help me understand why?

"Nope."

I had gotten tired of his one-word answers, so I asked, "Nick, if your presence doesn't add value to this company, do you think your absence will make a difference?"

He paused and responded, "Obi, I'll be honest with you. I just want to make my money and go home. I know my attitude has been shitty lately, but no, I don't think I could ever make a difference in a company so big."

"Nick, my people say, 'If you think you're too small to make a difference, you haven't spent a night with a mosquito'."

He laughed.

"You're smiling but it's true, Nick. Like the mosquitoes, you are never too insignificant to make a difference—positive or negative."

"Obi, they screwed up my legs when my girl and I went to Lake Minnetonka. I can't stand 'em. I can't imagine sleeping in a room full of mosquitoes."

"I have spent so many nights with them," I replied

"You have?"

"Yes."

"When you were in Africa?"

"Yes, and the ones in Africa give you something called malaria."

"What? You've had malaria? Are you serious?"

"Yes."

"Oh my God, Obi! Doesn't that kill people?"

"It does. Half a million people last year alone."

"Wow!"

"Yes. Trust me, Nick, those tiny mosquitoes make a big difference."

"I can't believe you've had malaria. That's scary."

"Malaria is not my point. My point is that you're not too small to make a difference. Trust me ..."

The coaching session ended with Nick requesting that I print out the quote about never being too small to make a difference. He wanted it on his desk as a reminder of the principle of adding value. Centuries ago, this principle was articulated by Jesus when he said,

"A good tree cannot produce bad fruit. And a bad tree

cannot produce good fruit."

You can only add value or make a positive difference if you have positive values within. This is why we spent the first five chapters on improving our inner values. You cannot give what you do not have.

In 1999, fifteen year old Jonathan James penetrated the computers of the US Department of Defense and intercepted thousands of emails. He also stole expensive software from NASA. Nine years later, another teenager, Dmitriy Guzner, did the same thing to the website of a multi-billion-dollar organization. Ten years later, in 2018, a sixteen year old Australian kid hacked Apple's corporate network and stole confidential information. You can be certain that in the next decade, another kid will cause great pain to a big corporation. There are other kids like Louis Braille, who invented the Braille system for the blind when he was just fifteen. We read of Philo Farnsworth, who was only fourteen when he designed the first fully electronic television, or the legendary Malala Yousafzai, who was shot in the head at only fifteen for her fight for equal rights to education. These kids prove that you are never too little to make a difference.

One "little" hacker in his parents' basement can take down a company's security infrastructure. One "little" employee with information on a corporation's financial gaps can floor a company listed on the Stock Exchange. One "little" whistleblower can bring irreparable damage to a government. In the same way, one dedicated employee can add tremendous value to a company and any sensible company would be foolish to lose them.

Does it mean that companies do not lose great talent? Of course not. Every day, great employees are let go from their companies where they have toiled and provided tremendous value. However, these employees leave large gaping holes that cannot be filled. They leave with what philosophers call "tacit knowledge".

Tacit knowledge is the type of knowledge that cannot be fully codified or written down. It is gained from years of experience, observation, imitation and practice. It is different from the knowledge you get from a classroom or training (explicit knowledge) and is arguably more useful. Some employers are catching up to the value in this intangible knowledge and are doing what they can to retain quality talent. These organizations recognize that their biggest asset is the tacit knowledge of their employees. Therefore, they provide incentives and raises as well as encourage knowledge management practices that allow their employers to be creative and innovative.

An argument can be made that America is one of the greatest countries because of its diversity. Think about the wealth of intangible knowledge that immigrants from all over the world have brought over the years. From the English to the French to the Irish to the Arabs and to you. Each immigrant brings with them a wealth of tacit knowledge that enriches the society. Albert Einstein, Dikembe Mutombo, Joseph Pulitzer, Arnold Schwarzenegger and the amazing Madeleine Albright were not born in America. However, there is no question that they have all shaped the American culture with their unique skills and tacit knowledge.

While you and I, the custodians of this knowledge, can bring a lot of value, we can also gain a lot in the process of giving this value. Think of it like a cycle. The first phase is valuing yourself and others (prior chapters). The second phase is giving value. The third phase of this cycle is receiving value. This third phase is out of the scope of this book, but I will give it brief consideration in the following paragraph.

Abraham Maslow, a renowned psychologist, described this third phase of the value cycle. In his paper on the human hierarchy of needs (published in 1943), he describes a model, depicted as a pyramid with five levels of basic human needs. I would encourage you to study those basic needs and see how adding value to your organization (and to other people) fulfils the basic human craving of self-actualization.

Having hopefully convinced you of the importance of adding value, I would like to show you how to. There is a science and method to this, broken down to the following steps:

1. *Understand the big picture (what problem is your company/ department trying to solve?).*
2. *Identify processes already created to achieve the big picture.*
3. *Identify gaps in those processes.*
4. *Fill in the gaps (or propose a fix for the gaps).*

The first step is to understand the purpose of your company or your department. This is what some people call "the big picture". Every company, every department, every program and every business is created to solve a problem. Figure out what problem your company is trying to solve—or better still, what problems your department or business solves. For instance, if you work for the customer service department of Samsung, the big picture of the company could be "creating a reliable brand associated with the best electronics, phones and operating system", while the goal of your department could be "enhancing Samsung's brand by providing the best customer service for our customers".

As you can see, the mission of your department supports the overall strategic mission of your organization. If you're unsure about your department's mission, ask your manager what problem you are trying to solve as a department or as a unit.

Once you do this, the next thing is to identify the existing processes that help your department or organization solve those problems. These processes would typically include aspects of your daily work or your job description. Again, if confused, ask your manager or a recruiter for a breakdown of your job description.

Once you have identified these processes, you are ready to add value.

Every organization or department suffers from some form of process paralysis. There are some things you do at work that could be done more efficiently or even done away with entirely! These processes were created as a means to an end but in so many organizations, they have become the end.

It could be something as simple as meetings. Are they necessary? Is the frequency optimal? Do they help everyone achieve the goals of the big picture? I have been in weekly meetings where everybody attends, few people talk, the others pretend to listen and then we all go back to our workstations. No actions taken! No strides made towards the big picture. The same things discussed the previous week were discussed in the current week and would most likely be discussed the following week. This is a good example of process paralysis. The immigrant interested in adding value must ask questions such as, is it beneficial to change the frequency of the meetings from weekly to biweekly? Is it advantageous to shorten them from an hour to thirty minutes per meeting? Or is there a way to improve productivity by taking notes and sending emails to everyone in attendance?

Tired of the meaningless, long meetings, I took the third option for one of my employers. I started summarizing the takeaways from every meeting. Each summary included action items and the names of those who were assigned to own the items. I would then send the summary to everyone, including those who did not make the meeting. The value of this was immediately noticeable. Our department became more efficient, our meeting times became shorter and my manager thanked me for it.

I started to apply the same process with Carolyn. Whenever we had one-on-one meetings, I would take notes and then shoot an email with a summary including discussion points, action items, due dates and so forth. We spent less time re-iterating things we already discussed and our meetings became more structured. My summaries also became structured, too. The first column had the items discussed. The second column had the people assigned to the items. The third had due dates for each action item. The last column had general comments.

My structured summary got adopted by other teams providing statuses for their meetings. It was a thing of pride for me to see others using what I created. It also came with some publicity that opened doors for me within the company and with our external clients. Again, see how this correlates with the method listed earlier:

1. *Understand the big picture/goal:* ***As a department, we are responsible for helping meet our commitments/obligations to the customer/company***
2. *Identify processes already created to achieve the big picture:* ***Weekly meetings were used to evaluate how well we were meeting those commitments/obligations***
3. *Identify gaps in those processes:* ***Our meetings were too long and the same topics were repeated over and over***

each week. This slowed us down with meeting our commitments/goals

4. *Fix the gaps:* ***Took notes and kept everyone updated on the status of our obligations/commitments***

Stopping at step 3 can have negative implications. For instance, so many people have eyes for gaps. They can easily spot issues, but have no intentions of presenting a solution. What they do not understand is that while it is easy to identify an anomaly, it takes a person of value to be creative enough to propose a fix. Beware of presenting a problem without proffering possible solutions—it has no constructive value and constitutes the difference between winners and mediocre people. This should be the same attitude outside work, in your relationships with others and even on social media. Do not get trapped into the mediocre mentality of complaining about things, people, governments, or institutions without suggesting real solutions.

In the example cited earlier, I did not whine about the repetition, length or lack of purpose of our meetings. I took a pen and went to work. This should be the same attitude for all immigrants of value.

I have discussed this concept with friends and family. Sometimes, they ask, "what if our processes have no gaps?"

My response has always been that I am yet to see a process that cannot be improved upon. However, I usually follow that up by proposing yet another easy way to add value to their places of work. It involves documenting what you do today. Capture your tacit knowledge with respect to your day-to-day work.

You will be surprised at how many on-the-job experiences, observations and processes you follow that are not documented.

You can create value by writing down these things during your down-time at work.

The value in this is that it will help new employees overcome their learning curve quicker. Many people get frustrated and quit their jobs because they feel overwhelmed. By documenting your tacit knowledge for even the simplest of tasks, you help them overcome this fear. Another value this provides is consistency and efficiency. Documenting what you do helps your coworkers do things uniformly and so improves efficiency.

For instance, I recall writing down steps I took when making outbound calls with my office phone. I wrote down the words I used for greeting the customer. I wrote down the exact words I used to advise them that the call may be recorded for quality assurance. I wrote down what to say if the call went to voicemail or if the customer picked up and said they did not want to talk to me. I presented what I wrote to my manager and peers who peer-reviewed it and made changes on what could improve in the wording.

My manager pushed for it to be adopted and we started using it as a team whenever we made outbound calls. Many organizations will welcome consistency, especially with messaging. It enriches the company's reputation, removes the confusion of inconsistencies and protects the company from potential legal ramifications.

When I became a manager, I encouraged those who worked for me to document their tacit knowledge of existing processes. They would develop their unique documents and we would have meetings where we would brainstorm and improve on their documentation. After the team agreed that the process met the expectations, I would draw a visual representation for the team and put the author's name on it. This way, the author felt some pride that his or her contribution was adopted by the department. This public recognition helped us improve our team's morale and made us more consistent and efficient.

Using the examples of meetings and process documentation, I hope you can see how normal and routine things can be improved and how you don't need permission to start improving some of them.

At this juncture, it is important to state that you may encounter criticism when adding value. Never take it personally – even if it is. The first thing to do is to listen up and figure out if the criticism is constructive or not. If it is not constructive, it is still important to listen, smile back, thank them for their thoughts and totally forget what they said. If it is constructive and helps improve on your work, make note of it and incorporate it into your process.

I remember one of my peers, a fellow immigrant, Raj, asking in a mocking tone, "Who told you to take notes during the meeting?"

I was not as hurt by the question as I was by the apparent mockery.

"Seriously, Obi, who told you to take notes and email everybody? We were all paying attention during the meeting and we know what happened. Did the manager ask you to write it down?"

"No, he didn't. I just thought it could be helpful. You don't think it is helpful?"

"I didn't say that. I just think it's funny," Raj said in his Indian accent, reigniting that wry smile.

If I had listened to my friend Raj, I would not have enjoyed some of the successes that I did. This is why it is extremely important to have confidence in yourself. If I didn't, I would have capitulated to his criticism and stopped doing what I believed was right. This is why we spent the preceding chapters discussing building confidence and value. You set yourself up for a life of mediocrity and failure if you only do things that fit with the expectations of others. You cannot please everyone and even the greatest people you can think of had fierce critics. As a matter of fact, the greater you become, the more criticism you will receive. However, I am yet to read of a great person who forsook the path of greatness because of their fear of criticism. Expect this criticism and let it fuel you in continuing to bring value.

In summary, it comes down to the following:

1. Having an eye for the big picture.
2. Understanding what problem your company or department solves.
3. Understanding the process by which your job or your department's efforts helps solves this problem.
4. Finding holes, redundancies or inefficiencies in these processes.
5. Taking actions within your power to solve these process gaps.
6. Documenting your tacit knowledge on work processes.
7. Ignoring criticism and trusting your judgement.

Transgression of this principle:

After thirty-seven years in power, in November of 2017, ninety-three year old President Robert Mugabe was forced out of office in utter disgrace. He had been the only president of Zimbabwe since it gained its independence from the British in 1980. Heralded as the great liberator and one who would emancipate his people, Mugabe only succeeded in making his country worse than it was during its colonial era. He violently cracked down on protests, tortured his opponents, suppressed the press and under his watch, the unemployment rate in Zimbabwe skyrocketed to a dizzying eighty percent! Despite a promising start to his political career, which bore striking parallels to the great Nelson Mandela, Mugabe refused to add value to the lives of his people who put their trust and hope in him. Like most tyrants, history will not look kindly on his legacy and, he will go down in infamy despite having nearly forty years to add value to the lives of Zimbabweans.

Observance of this principle:

Funded by China's Jiangsu group and other public-private partnerships, musical sensation—Akon used his influence to create the "Akon Lighting Africa" project, which has brought solar power to fifteen African countries as at the time of the publication of this book. A massive project that solves an urgent need; funding was always going to be an issue. However, the Senegalese American star got around this hurdle by partnering with the Chinese investment group and a bunch of other stakeholders to bring much needed electricity to the communities in those fifteen countries. The impact of his initiative was both immediate and immense for those communities. Their farmers started storing their crops longer than before. Their women could make more money by selling their goods well into the nights as the streets were lit up. The roads became safer at night as streetlights made it tougher for thieves to harass people. Akon found a way to improve security, safety and jobs in those countries. He identified the gaps in their fledgling economies and utilized his celebrity influence in partnering with stakeholders to address those gaps. To this end, he embodies the principle of adding value.

CHAPTER 7

The Winning Mentality

"Eneke the bird says that since men have learned to shoot without missing, he has learned to fly without perching."

- Chinua Achebe in *Things Fall Apart*

If you do not change how you think, you will never be able to change your circumstances. Everything you have learned in the course of your life—up until this point—will amount to nothing, if it does not force you to change how you think. It isn't what you read that counts. It comes down to what you think about what you read—and how that challenges your preconceived notions. King Solomon—widely regarded as one of the smartest kings in history—agreed with this truth, when he wrote, "As a man thinks in his heart, so he is". Second century Roman emperor, Marcus Aurelius, also said, "We become what we think about. A man's life is what his thoughts make of it." And even, the well-respected British author, James Allen, wrote, "You are today where your thoughts have brought you. You will be tomorrow where your thoughts take you." These great thinkers and many others, understand the power of thought—and its role in changing our circumstances.

All the great technology and comforts we enjoy today, were possible hundreds of years ago. Why didn't people in the Middle Ages make videos, use GPS or fly airplanes? These technologies were not recently created by God nor did they evolve from nothing. The reason we enjoy these things today—and they didn't—is because men and women started to think differently and in so doing, changed their circumstances. The things we call 'inventions' or 'discoveries' have always been there. We have only recently learned how to think about—and apply them—differently. Think about this: the mobile phone in your hand is more powerful than the computers that helped take Neil Armstrong to the moon in July of 1969. And that same mobile phone will become obsolete in a few years. Our world is fast evolving because so many men and women are changing and challenging their thought patterns. They are not more educated than people in the Middle Ages; but they are thinking a lot differently. The same principle is true with our personal lives and circumstances. If you do not change how you think, you'll never be able to change your circumstances.

One of the greatest tragedies in life is finding yourself at the right place, at the right time—and yet failing to grasp the significance of the opportunity in front of you. This happens more often than we think. We sometimes forget that, being at the right place at the right time, isn't enough. Without the right mentality or mindset; it amounts to nothing. You wouldn't even notice it. The winning mentality gives the right perspective to our current situations and helps us make the most of it. There is hardly anything more unfortunate, than having the stars of the universe align in your favor, and not have the good sense to recognize its significance. As a matter of fact, it is better to have a winning mindset than to be in the right place at the right time. This is because, a winning mentality can turn the wrong place into the right place and transform the seemingly wrong time into the perfect time.

The story of the immigrant janitor—Frank Baez—narrated in Chapter 4, captures the essence of the winning mentality.

Despite his misfortunes, he made the most of his situation, adapted to his new country, brushed up his communication skills, took other concrete steps to improve himself, and kept a most cheerful attitude while doing these. He didn't whine about his lack of command of the English language, or his poverty level. He didn't blame his family for not putting him in the best position to succeed in life, nor compare himself to his more successful peers. Frank kept pushing hard while remaining grateful for the little he had.

Michael Faraday became one of the most influential scientists in history because of his revolutionary works in demonstrating how magnetism affects rays of light. He laid the foundation of 'electromagnetic field' in physics that is still relevant today. However, what many do not remember is that he came from abject poverty and received very little formal education. His poor beginnings did not lead him to self-pity, nor stop him from educating himself and making the most of his life.

Sir Isaac Newton is also regarded as one of the most influential scientists of all time. His laws of motion laid the foundation for classical mechanics and are still relevant today. What many do not remember is that Isaac was born prematurely and lost his father three months before he was born. His widowed mom did not like his love for Math and pushed him to be a farmer—an occupation he hated. However, despite the universe seemingly conspiring against the young Isaac; he made the most of himself.

Julius Nyerere was one of twenty six children and herded cattle before becoming the first president of Tanzania. Kwame Nkrumah was born to an illiterate and impoverished family, but rose to become the first president of Ghana. Jomo Kenyatta—the first President of Kenya—was poor at school and had to drop out. However, this setback did not stop him as much as it spurred him. We can go on and on about great people who overcame incredible odds thanks to their winning mentality. Ellen Johnson Sirleaf, the great Nelson Mandela, Martin Luther King Jr, Mahatma Gandhi and Rosa Parks. These people did not let their difficult circumstances dictate the outcome of their lives. They had what is regarded in pop culture as 'the mamba mentality' – a relentless quest to be better and to seize the moment. They fought, they scraped and they adapted. Paraphrasing Julius Cesar; they came, they saw, they conquered.

Adaptation and a winning mentality are necessary for conquest. You find both traits in most winners. It doesn't matter if they are minimum wage workers, janitors scrubbing toilets or inmates locked up in secure facilities. Their past doesn't matter. They always make the most of the cards life has dealt them, and they eventually actualize their God-given potential. On the other hand, you can have all the money and power within your grasp. But with a crappy attitude, all of that wealth and power amount to nothing and are soon gone.

In the corporate world, the reason employers ask for your resume is to get an idea of your accomplishments. The reason they invite you for an interview, is to get an insight into your personality, mentality and general attitude. They pose situational questions, asking how you handled trying dilemmas. They ask about a tough co-worker from the past, or a former boss, and how you reacted to their difficulties or handled their eccentricities. They ask what motivates you and where you see yourself in the next five years. Good interviewers pay attention to the content and structure of your answers in order to understand your mentality. They know the immense value of a great mentality and have turned down qualified people because of this. A great attitude trumps accomplishments any day. And as Zig Zigler put it,

"Your attitude, not your aptitude, will determine your altitude".

Many employers would rather work with someone with a great attitude, but lacks certain hard skills, than one with a poor attitude, albeit possessing all the hard skills listed in the job description. The reason is simple. It is easier to teach hard skills than it is to teach a positive mentality. This makes a winning mentality much more valuable than any college degree or certification the world of academia has to offer. Besides, the person with a healthy mentality is teachable, will work hard and will foster a healthy team atmosphere.

True personal and professional success can only be achieved by the deliberate formation of a winning mentality, and this mentality is the culmination of all the principles you have been exposed to in this book. This mentality embodies the mental attitude necessary to succeed as an immigrant. It involves being open, teachable and adaptable like Eneke the bird.

Understanding your innate powers and your new environment is of essence in adapting. Think about the most feared Sub-Saharan African beast, the lion. It is, without doubt, one of the most successful animals in our jungles. It is so successful that it is considered the king of the jungle.

The Igbos call it *Agu*—a name synonymous with royalty, power and success.

However, the lion is nowhere as big as the elephant, nor is it as heavy as a hippo. The lion is not as tall as the Somalian camels or the Sahel giraffes of West Africa. It is not as quick as the cheetah or the pronghorn antelope. The lion is not even as smart as our African monkeys or the ravens. How then could this cat rule the jungle? Why does it not shrink at the sight of all these animals that are stronger, smarter, taller, heavier and quicker than it? Why do those animals fear the lion, enough to allow it such dominion over them?

What makes the lion see the elephant that is much bigger and heavier than it is, and not run away? Why does it see a hippo, and think "breakfast"? Why does it see an antelope that is way taller than it is; and instead of processing "fear", it processes "lunch"? It all comes down to mentality. One can have all the smarts or college degrees in the world and still be dominated by people with little to no education. Again, it all comes down to the mentality of the person or the people. A winning mentality pushes you beyond your expected limitations. It is the reason the lion is still the dominant wild beast today; 800,000 years after it first appeared as the Panthera Leo. It does not make excuses for its lack of height or speed or smarts. Instead, it leverages what it has. There is a lot we can learn from this cat to apply in the jungles of corporate America.

Let us start by evaluating five habits we must give up to truly have this winning mentality:

- **Wasting time and resources:** The winning mentality calls for a complete rejection of any form of time wasting. The lion is timely and deliberate with its hunt. It instinctively employs a business timing and prioritization model called WSJF. WSJF is an acronym for Weighted Shortest Job First and involves the calculation of business value, time factors, duration, risk, opportunities, effort and other factors required for a specific job or contract. So many corporations use this model in deciding what work to do first, when to do it and what to avoid. In the same way, the king of the jungle instinctively weighs the value, risk, opportunity, time and duration effort required in capturing its prey before going for it. This inborn WSJF model prompts the lion to go after only two little zebras instead of an adult elephant, even if the elephant will provide more meat. This instinctive model is crucial to the lion's dominance in the wild. And just as it cannot be successful without this timing and prioritization, you cannot be successful if you are unable to manage and prioritize your time.

Time is the most valuable asset that you have. While we live in a society that treats money as more valuable, money only ranks fourth on the list of life's most valuable assets. Therefore, wasting time is four times as expensive as wasting money. Planning, prioritizing and all the time management disciplines discussed in Chapter One will help you master this concept.

I know many people going through unimaginable stress because of the feeling of having so much to do and not enough time. Some of the same people spend an inordinate amount of time on their phones or in idle talk with friends. At the end of the day, they stay up worried and feeling defeated. In the long run, they could battle with a litany of stress-related diseases. Mastering time management is crucial to managing stress and feeling accomplished.

I have noticed that whenever I get more work done or goals accomplished, I sleep better at night. Activities like scrolling through social media platforms, reading the news all the time and even idle talk with your friends can be addictive. Because they are so addictive, they take away most of our time.

A corollary to managing time is setting long term goals and following them up with short term habits to achieve these goals. Some of you already do this. I know a lot of immigrants who gave up short term gratification and went back to school because they see the long-term play. I know others who have given up extra pay or managerial positions so that they could have time to start a side business or spend with their children. Whatever decisions you make, keeping an eye on the big picture helps you make the most of your time and avoid needless delays. Renowned project management author Don Reinersten once wrote,

"If you only quantify one thing, quantify the cost of delay."

This is true for both managing projects and managing our limited time.

While time is our most valuable asset, the principle of time management also calls for having a big picture perspective when it comes to resource management. This perspective will trigger habits such as investing, especially in a 401K at work. Most corporations match your contributions up to a certain percentage of your income. But it all starts with the discipline of putting something away every paycheck to ensure that your future self enjoys some financial freedom. Only those who make it a priority to value their limited time and resources would make this discipline a habit. Other habits, such as gambling, excessive partying, taking unnecessary loans or living beyond your means, will limit your success.

Balance is of the essence.

- **Excuses:** As stated earlier, the lion does not make excuses for its lack of height or speed or smarts. In the same vein, the winning mentality calls for giving up excuses completely, whether valid or not. Is the lion smaller than the elephant? Yes. Does that stop the lion from eating it for lunch? No! People with a winning mindset never have excuses or blame other people for their woes. They take control of their lives irrespective of the disadvantages or obstacles they face. Whatever you become or do not become is on you. It is not on your parents or the government or your country. Any contrary train of thought constitutes a victim mentality. This does not mean that our parents or government or society do not play a part in our circumstances. However, it is one thing to suffer an injustice and another to wallow in self-pity or mediocrity because of the injustice. Injustice or discrimination are not sufficient to color the mindset of winners. Think about it this way; if you found out that your spouse was cheating on you, would you react by cheating back on them? The one with the victim mentality would get depressed and then sleep with someone else to get back at their spouse. The one with the victor mentality would not let the infidelity stain his or her character. The victim makes excuses for their cheating using rationales such as "my spouse cheated, so it's okay for me to cheat". The victor makes no excuses. The same attitude applies to working in corporate America. There are so many valid excuses not to give your best. You roll your eyes at your manager because they said something unprofessional. You falsify your timecard because others are doing it. You come into work late because others come in late. You cuss at work because your coworkers do. You have become a person of excuses instead of a person of excellence. Does the lion eat grass because the giraffe does? Does it settle for grass when all its prey have run away? It stays true to what it is (Know Yourself) and changes its environment by advancing to where it can find prey (Grow Yourself). This truth was best articulated in a famous African proverb that goes:

"No matter the economy of the jungle, the lion will never eat grass."

To effectively avoid the victim mentality, you must know yourself, grow yourself and imbibe the disciplines in Chapter Four. You have the power to change your circumstance. We all do. It is important that you believe this and approach life from this point of view. That being said, you cannot control everything just like the lion cannot control the routine of its prey. However, differentiating between changing your circumstance and controlling things outside your control is important. The key is to focus on improving yourself and making the best of the cards you are dealt with.

- **Self-Doubt:** The winning mentality calls for self-confidence. Anything short of a healthy dose of self-confidence will stunt your success. Even the untamed lion understands this concept and has leveraged it to retain its royalty status in the jungles of Africa. It would be extinct today if it doubted its strength and dominance. Someone once defined hell this way:

"On your last day on earth, the person you became will meet the person you could have become."

You cannot live your life doubting yourself. Every day is an opportunity to grow in some way, shape or form. Chapters Three and Four delve into this concept to encourage you to become all you can be. Besides stopping you from attaining personal goals, self-doubt also makes you think you cannot make any difference in the outside world. Self-doubt is so dangerous that it has stopped many from realizing their full potential and has driven others to depression.

It is crucial that you know your worth. About four years ago, I remember pushing an employee, John, to apply for a position that I believed he was qualified for. While managing him, I could see how hardworking, ethical and reliable he was. If he got the position, we would have been on the same leadership level. I spoke so highly of John and I remember talking to a director about the value he would bring to the company if he got a promotion. I spoke about how knowledge from his bachelor's degree and his overall attitude would be huge assets for us. He also had a family and I knew that ten or eleven dollars an hour would not be sustainable in the long run.

"We are going to lose him if we don't entrust him with more," I said to the director.

"Obi, you really like this guy. He must have made a good impression on you," he responded.

"He is that good, Aaron," I replied.

I was so invested in helping John succeed, like all servant leaders should—and we had become friends. John eventually got the position and our friendship became even stronger.

During one of our conversations, the subject of salary came up and John revealed what he was making at his new role. I found out he was making five thousand dollars more than I was, despite having no experience in the position. This realization opened my eyes! I realized that I was putting so much of my efforts into becoming the best servant leader that I could be, that I had neglected my personal interests. I tell this story to demonstrate why you must never let your servant leadership lead to servility. You must not forget yourself while looking out for the best interests of others. The greatest command Jesus gave his followers was that they love their neighbors as themselves. Not *more* than themselves. My interactions with John taught me not only to value myself, but to never take the first compensation package offered to me. People rarely offer you their best deals at first. If you hired someone to clean your house and you had a hundred dollars to spare, would you offer them the hundred dollars when you know so many people get paid fifty dollars to do the same work? It is the same concept in corporate America. Employers rarely offer you what you are worth the first time. They have a budget and usually offer you the lower limits of that budget. Irrespective of how amazing the first offer is, I have learned to use sentences like:

"Thank you for your generous offer. I'm so excited! Is it okay if I review this with my family and get back to you within the week?"

This affords you some time to think about what you could use to bargain for more. Check the market rate for people doing a similar job, factor in your moving costs or other costs you think you will incur by taking the job. These will help you make an informed counter offer.

As you can tell, a glaring trait of people who doubt themselves is they always say yes. It is important to say yes when we can, but we must be cognizant of the fact that no is a legitimate answer. Saying no is not rude—especially when you do so by providing reasons. Self-doubt and lack of confidence in your value can be real impediments to appreciating the wisdom of the philosophy of no. People with a winning mentality cannot and should not say yes all the time.

- **Ego**: The person with the winning mentality has a healthy dose of humility. Humility does not negate self-confidence, but supplements it. For instance, the lion knows it cannot take on certain animals on its own, so it hunts in prides or groups of other lions. Its self-confidence does not descend into ego. Otherwise, it would hunt an elephant alone and probably get crushed. Furthermore, we do not hear the lion roaring while trying to catch its prey. As wild and untamed as it is, it knows the importance of silence and that being loud and noisy will hinder its ability to catch prey. The lion is extremely humble! It is aware of its weaknesses and knows how to turn them into strengths.

This humility, which has enabled the lion to succeed for so long in the wild, can also help you succeed in the corporate world. One way to leverage humility is the use of job or career coaches. This concept involves asking a manager at your workplace—not necessarily *your* manager—to help you with your career goals. Most people in management will feel flattered that you have asked them to mentor you and take you under their wings, but it takes letting go of one's ego to seek this mentorship. However, once you do, you will learn areas you need to improve upon and, like the lion, you will enjoy much more success. These managers or directors are usually busy, but a fifteen minute discussion every other week is time well invested and will do you a lot of good. There are a lot of examples on how you can leverage humility in the workplace, but this mentorship example is easily applicable to almost any workplace.

Still on the subject of ego, many men from the motherland see themselves as superior to women. It is common in many patriarchal societies and I had a similar mentality coming to America. We never say it out loud, but we assume that when it comes to certain activities, we are better than our women. However, I let go of that flawed mentality thanks to experience, study and a thorough introspection of myself. I am not smarter, better or greater than any woman or any man. As has been repeated throughout this book, the winning mentality calls for seeing yourself as a god among other gods. Chapter Two delves into this concept and I recommend re-reading it if you still struggle with letting go of this disposition.

Homophobia is also another cultural bias many of us, migrants, come with. Our cultural norms and religious inclinations frown on the gay culture. However, having a winning mentality means that you must see them as your equals. Do not let your ego or bias cause you to isolate yourself from them or treat them as less than equals. The same goes for everyone you interact with. There is always something to learn, even from those who hate you and discriminate against you. If you pay close attention to them, you will be blown away at how much they have to teach you.

- **Bad Company:** You never see lions hanging out with donkeys. That would be an aberration. You never read of eagles chilling with chickens. If you did, you would think such an eagle is naïve of its strengths. In the same vein, successful immigrants must be careful about the quality of people they surround themselves with. Surrounding yourself with people who are toxic, mediocre and who spend most of their time in idle talk will hurt you more than you know. The winning mentality calls for us to be friendly with them, but avoid being close friends with them. Build relationships with people who will challenge you and help you grow as explained in Chapter Five.

This mentality also calls for giving up the need to be validated. This need is the primary reason people forge useless friendships at work and outside work. It is said that the lion doesn't lose sleep over the opinions of sheep. It doesn't care about or crave their validation, acceptance or love. If you do not give up this craving to be validated or loved, you will surround yourself with people who do not foster your growth. They may have good intentions, but they will end up pulling you down. I know people who told close friends they wanted to quit their jobs or take a break off school and their friends encouraged them to, without knowing the full circumstances. Of course there are valid reasons to quit your job or school, but you need a support system that would delve a little more into the rationale of your decisions before weighing in. You do not need an inner circle of yes men, but friends who would challenge and encourage you simultaneously.

In an age of technology, bad company is not confined to the physical office or real world. It extends to the virtual world. Social media has grown substantially in relevance. Its positive impact is remarkable, but so is its negative impact. Like fire, you must learn to master it, otherwise it can burn down all your accomplishments. Employers, landlords, coworkers and even the government now look into your social media activities. At the time of writing this book, there are concrete plans being made by the US government to require immigrants, applying to come to the US, to submit five years of social media history.

One seemingly trivial post could potentially hurt your chances and tarnish your reputation irreparably. Rebuilding this tarnished reputation is as daunting as rebuilding a building razed down by a fire. Unless your goals depend on social media, minimize its use and guard your peace from its polluting influence.

Speaking of polluting influences and reputation, if you drink at all; be mindful of those you drink with. Alcohol and other substances impair your judgement and decision making. Besides the obvious health and criminal risks (such as driving while intoxicated), there are smartphones everywhere that could capture your impaired judgement at a private or public event. These pictures or media files can resurface anytime and do you great harm. With the right company, this risk is greatly minimized.

The workplace is filled with so many people who genuinely feel persecuted. Some of them truly are, others do this to gain attention or avoid self-responsibility. They constantly blame others for everything wrong and walk around with a "the whole world is against me" mentality. They feel attacked when confronted with gaps in their work. They in turn attack coworkers or friends who seek to help them grow. What is worse? Because they expect to always get sympathy from others, they become difficult to work with when they don't get it. For you to succeed in corporate America—and in life—you must be careful about the pitfalls of this mentality. As a matter of fact, you must reject it completely.

Randy Paush in *The Last Lecture* said,

"It's not about the cards you're dealt, but how you play the hand."

Not getting your way or being denied opportunities you think you deserve is no justification for imbibing this victim mentality. You are not a victim. You are a victor—just like the lion. Leaving your country, your people, your friends and family is not something losers do. It is not what victims do! Learning a new language and transitioning from a collectivist to an individualistic culture is not for the faint hearted. You have overcome obstacles so many people in the western world have never encountered and here you are in America, making a way for yourself and your family. Do you remember the volume of paperwork you or your parents had to fill in? How many interviews you and your family had to pass? How many rigorous background checks and scrutiny you had to go through? How many restless nights and insecurities you had to overcome? There is no job in the world as difficult as what you have encountered already. No school or college prepares you for what you have overcome already. All of these make you victorious and it is crucial you keep this winning mentality all the time. Nobody and no job should ever scare you—just like no animal or beast ever scares the lion. Like the lion, you should know your limitations and leverage them effectively.

Every new job comes with some learning—even for the most qualified people. All you need is training on the job and time, and you will be just as good as anyone else.

One of my managers used to say,

"If you gave me six months at any job in the world, I would be proficient at it. If you gave me one year at the same job, I would be an expert!"

I have found this to be true and would not make these assertions if they did not work for me or for my friends. In 2018, a young immigrant I know, applied to become an engineer for a US government contractor. He had never been to engineering school nor held such a position before. However, he read the job description and was convinced he could bring value.

The young man told the interviewer that even though he lacked the technical expertise of an engineer and had only taken one class in writing codes, he was dependable and efficient (Chapter 1 - Time Management). The young man asked the interviewer what immediate issues his company was having. The interviewer listed some of them and the young man quickly described ways that he could help fix the flaws in the company's engineering processes. He told the interviewer that he had helped fix broken processes in his previous job and could repeat the same methods with this company (Chapter 6 - Adding Value). He gave him other tangible examples of how he could add value, referencing his success in school and his other certifications (Chapter 4 - Know Yourself. Grow Yourself). He convinced him that he was not worried about his ability to learn the technical aspects of the job (Chapter 3 - Self Confidence) or get along with his peers and blend in with the company's culture (Chapter 2 - Servant Leadership).

He was hired on the spot and asked if he could start the

following week. The young man thanked him but told him how much he valued his relationship with his employer at the time. As such, he would like to give them at least three weeks, to find a replacement for him (Chapter 5 – Building Meaningful Relationships).

The interviewer was impressed. He said they would wait three weeks for him if that was what he needed. The young man went on to become a successful aerospace engineer and accepted other roles within the organization by applying the principles in this book. The same principles helped him become president of the engineering council for his state. I tell this true story because I know the same can be true for you! Like every science, applying the same steps should lead to similar outcomes.

Courtney, a beautiful African American lady at a previous job, ran up to me in tears. She hugged me tight and I hugged her back.

"What's wrong, Courtney? Is everything okay? Are you okay?" I asked. It was the first time she gave me a hug.

"No, Obi. I'm not … I'll never be okay. They hate us, Obi. They hate you."

"What do you mean, Courtney?"

"They hate us!" she continued. "What do we ever have to do to be good enough?"

"What do you mean?" I asked again as I led her away from the office floor.

She narrated how two female coworkers were discussing my recent promotion in the mother's room. "You need to hear how they were talking about you, Obi."

"Who?"

"Maggie and Lisa. They were in the mother's room and did not know I could hear them. I left my charger in the room and when I went to get it, I could see those two bitches talking. I knew something was up."

"Don't call them bitches."

"That's what they are, Obi. Bitches!"

"Okay. What did they say? What were they talking about?"

"They said you got the promotion not because you did well in your interview, they say you got it because you are black and they don't have any black managers here. So the company's trying to look good by promoting you."

"Hmm."

"Yeah, Obi. They say you don't know anything and that they're smarter than you. Lisa said she heard your interview was messed up and that she will quit."

"Quit?"

"Yeah, Obi, can you believe these clowns? Just because you got the program manager job."

"It's okay, Courtney," I replied.

"No, it's not!" she cut in. "You have to go to HR. Obi, you have to. This is not fair. What do we have to do to be good enough for these people?"

"It's okay."

"No, it's not. We win, they say it's because we are black. We lose, they say it's because we are black. Like, seriously, what do we have to do?"

Courtney was in tears and sniffling. I had been doing a poor job at consoling her. I looked around the room we were seated in. Usually, there was a box of tissue but on this day, there was none. I could see the hurt in her eyes. I could tell that the conversation she overheard triggered the sentiments many minorities feel in this country—that feeling of having the society and institutions stacked against you.

Courtney's concerns were real. Her fears were a reflection of our reality. Some of you may have felt the same type of injustice. However, it is important to take care how you react to these injustices.

While it is important to confront any and all discriminatory actions, you must never walk around feeling sorry for yourself. While you cannot control the actions of others, you have complete control over your reaction to their ignorance. Their actions may be defeating, but your mentality cannot be defeated. Their actions may be hate-filled, but you cannot let hate into your soul. Their actions could be racist, but you cannot feel sorry for yourself.

Once you succumb to this mentality, you close the doors you fought so hard to open in the preceding chapters. As immigrants, some of these injustices are not alien to you. Back home, you are probably used to a government being chosen from a specific tribe and your tribe ignored. You are probably used to bosses back home denying you or your loved ones promotions because you are not from their ethnic group. You have probably experienced the need to know people in order to get a shot at a job, despite being qualified. Some of you may have experienced an inability to marry someone you love because their people think your tribe is inferior. You probably know people who have been mercilessly beaten by African law enforcement for speaking their minds. The list of discriminatory actions you or people you love have endured is as long as the Nile! However, these painful experiences did not make you feel sorry for yourself or wallow in self-pity. You survived amid all the corruption without being corrupted in the process. This is exactly what it means to have a winning mentality. Do not lose this and fall into a victim mentality just because you're in America.

Carry that winning mentality and authenticity here. Not just in how you think, but how you dress and conduct yourself. I have been mocked in the past by some of my peers for wearing blazers or dress shirts, tucked into well-ironed trousers and donning polished dress shoes. One of them said,

"You dress like Obama but you make only ten dollars an hour."

He was ignorant of the fact that our people dress to the magnitude of the occasion. A job is not to be taken lightly. It is a big deal. There is no reason anyone should convince you to wear pajamas or dress down to your workplace, even if you're just at the entry level. You would not wear that at your job in Africa, you shouldn't here either.

Preserve that authenticity even if they mock you. The winning mentality dictates that you do not take anything they say personally. Focus on your goals and have a dress code that matches those goals.

Beyond your dressing, authenticity is important. I cannot over-emphasize how important it is to be true to yourself and your values. People can usually tell when you are fake and superficial. Be genuinely proud of your roots without feeling inferior. Be actively aware of injustice without having it color your opinion of the other race. Be open to criticism without being defensive or sorry for yourself. Dress for the occasion even if you are the only one doing it. Work through obstacles with a smile on your face even though you know the obstacles are man-made. These paradoxes are the stuff winners are made of!

In summary, a winning mentality is the crowning jewel of all the success principles we have discussed so far. A lack of this mindset can invalidate the principles in the preceding chapters. It all comes down to:

1. Giving up bad habits such as wasting time, excuses, doubting yourself, ego and bad company
2. Being teachable and adaptable
3. Being authentic to yourself and your past/history/culture
4. Being authentic your future goals
5. Taking responsibility for your mistakes without taking criticisms personally
6. Ignoring self-pity and any thoughts of victimhood
7. Mastering the paradox of winners

Transgression of this principle:

For many decades, Kodak was the world leader in cameras, film equipment and photographic services. Such was their dominance that even today, the phrase "Kodak Moment" is still a popular expression for a memorable moment. However, by the late 90s, digital imaging technology was replacing the film paper technology and Kodak sought to drag down this new technology. The interesting thing is that Kodak was actually the first to invent the digital camera. Steve Sasson, an engineer with the company, developed it in 1975. Rather than exploit his creation, Kodak suppressed it because of the threat they assumed it posed. They lacked the element of adaptability that all winners need to have to be successful. When they realized their mistake, other players had eaten away from their ninety percent market share. By 2013, Kodak only escaped bankruptcy by selling its patents off for 525 million dollars. Its inability to adapt to the changing times proved to be its downfall.

Observance of this principle:

One of the best disciples of the principle of honing a winning mentality is Daymond John. The Black American businessman is best known for being the founder, president and CEO of FUBU. However, his path to success was anything but smooth. While many ten year olds fall apart after a divorce, Daymond took on a part-time job handing out flyers, at two dollars an hour, to support his mom. In high school, he participated in a program that allowed him to work a full-time job while attending school on an alternating weekly basis, which he credits with instilling in him an entrepreneurial spirit. When done with school, he started FUBU in his mother's basement after she taught him how to sew. He recruited his childhood friends and together they began sewing the FUBU logo onto hockey jerseys, sweatshirts, and tee-shirts. Unsure how to popularize the shirts beyond selling them on the streets, he put his winning mentality to good use. Daymond loaned about ten of the hockey jerseys to rappers for their music videos and got product placements in about thirty videos. FUBU became popular and people thought it was a large brand name, not knowing it was being made in the basement of Daymond's mom's house. In 1993, he convinced mainstream rapper, LL Cool J, an old neighborhood friend, to wear a FUBU T-shirt for a promotional campaign and a commercial. LL agreed and even used the words FUBU or "For Us By Us" in his rap lyrics. That was the true breakthrough for Daymond who received $300,000 in orders as well as offers and orders from Macy's. To fulfil the large orders that were coming fast and furious, Daymond went to twenty-seven different banks for loans. They all turned him down. However, Daymond was not one to take rejection to heart or let it dampen his winning mentality. Like Eneke the bird, he was open, teachable and adaptable to the lessons of life. So he turned to his mother and urged her to mortgage their home. She believed in him and mortgaged it in order to fund the large orders. That gamble proved to be immensely successful. FUBU has made over six billion dollars in sales and Daymond continues to be an inspiration to a lot of entrepreneurs on the importance of inculcating a winning mentality.

Epilogue

"Raise your words, not your voice. It is rain that grows flowers, not thunder."

- Rumi

As an immigrant, the greatest thing you could do for yourself and for those around you is to become a person of value. This involves focusing on personal development and growing your God-given talents so as to become the best possible version of yourself. On the other hand, the worst thing you could do is allow yourself to become a child of chance, circumstance and fear in America. Even animals do not let chance, circumstances and fear rule them. They improve their survival chances and overall circumstances by migrating or confronting the enemy. They may fear the danger posed by animals higher up the food chain, but they know enough to take steps to mitigate the danger. How much more you, an immigrant who has overcome strife, hardships, discrimination and cultural shock, to make it here?

You are not barred from attaining success in corporate America or in life because of your color or heritage. You are barred by how you respond to these injustices. The secret is choosing how to react. And you can start today. Victims argue with life while victors embrace life. Victims believe they are helpless, while victors know they can control their lives. Victims wallow in self-pity while victors laugh at their oppressors.

Victims blame everyone else for their misfortunes while victors affirm self-responsibility.

However, having this badass mentality does not suffice. Just like faith without works is dead, a winning mentality without actions is cremated.

The principles of time management, servant leadership, self-confidence, self-growth, building meaningful relationships and adding value to others, combined with the winning mentality, will awaken the immense power inside of you! You will not only be a financial success, but will have fulfilment and purpose—outcomes that money cannot buy.

I recommend that you study these principles over and over until they become part and parcel of your routine. Once they become habit, you will be amazed at how much power you have! How much control you have over your circumstances and how everything starts falling into place.

Made in the USA
Monee, IL
08 November 2026

67944875R00080